LIBRARY CATALOGING:
A Guide for a Basic Course

by
John Phillip Immroth
and
Jay E. Daily

The Scarecrow Press, Inc.
Metuchen, N.J.   1971

The Library of Congress Cataloged the Original Printing of
This Title as:

Immroth, John Phillip.
 Library cataloging: a guide for a basic course. by John
Phillip Immroth and Jay E. Daily. Metuchen. N. J.,
Scarecrow Press, 1971.

 202 p. illus. 22 cm.

 Includes bibliographies.

 1. Cataloging—Outlines, syllabi, etc.   I. Daily, Jay Elwood, joint
author.   II. Title.

Z693.I 45   025.3′02′02   72–147066
ISBN 0–8108–0396–8   MARC

Library of Congress   71 [20–2]

PREFACE

The purpose of this guide is to aid the beginning library student in understanding the organization of library materials. This guide is intended to be used with the first course in cataloging and classification. It is not meant to replace either a textbook or a course. It should be a supplement to either of these.

The guide is made up of individual units of study. Each unit contains the following:

1) A narrative introduction--designed to be both an introduction and summary of the material covered in the unit.

2) A detailed topical outline of the material covered in the unit.

3) A list of basic readings--including citations to the standard textbooks.

4) A list of enrichment readings--designed to supplement the material covered in each unit.

5) Individual worksheets for each part of the course.

6) Additional instructional materials, including sample catalog cards.

This guide is divided into two main parts: descriptive analysis and subject analysis. Descriptive analysis includes the basic principles and practices of the physical description of materials. Subject analysis deals with the subject indexing and arrangement of materials.

The main objectives of the first course in cataloging should be: 1) to introduce the student to basic concepts, purposes and theories of cataloging and classification; 2) to help him understand the organization and functions of the library catalog; 3) to make him aware of the job of

the cataloger and the organization of the cataloging department and its relationship to other departments of the library; and 4) to examine the basic reference sources the
cataloger uses in performing his work and to teach the
student to use them.

CONTENTS

Part 2: Subject Analysis

INTRODUCTION

Technical services may be defined as those library activities which are performed in areas not accessible to the public. Traditionally technical services are divided into three separate processes and departments. These processes are acquisitions, cataloging, and serials. Acquisitions means the buying of library materials, the exchanging of library materials, and the receiving of library materials as gifts. Acquisitions may be thought of as the three "B's"--buying, bartering, and begging. Cataloging is the process of technical services which deals with the indexing and arranging of library materials. Serials is concerned with the acquisition and cataloging of subscription-type materials.

There are many types of material which must be processed by technical services. The most common type of material is the book. A book, or as librarians call it, a monograph, may be defined as a work, collection or other writing dealing with a particular subject or subjects. Monographs differ from serials, which are defined as publications issued in successive installments at regular or irregular intervals and intended to be continued indefinitely. Periodicals are one common type of serials. A work may be considered to be a periodical if it is not cataloged and classified and is simply arranged alphabetically with other periodicals or magazines. Some serials will be cataloged and classified and shelved with either the reference books or the circulating books. Pamphlets are another type of library material which is not cataloged or classified but rather filed alphabetically by subject. The modern library has many other types of materials which are called non-book or special materials. These include records, motion pictures, filmstrips, slides, framed prints, and even machine-readable data such as computer tapes.

The following flowchart demonstrates the basic processes of technical services for a book or monograph. The first step in this process may be called the request for a particular title. A librarian or a patron may request that a particular book be in the collection. The second step is the selection process. Usually the ac-

quisitions librarian must decide if the library wishes to
buy the requested item.   If the acquisitions librarian de-
cides that the title should be added to the collection, the
third step called searching must be done.   Searching is
simply checking to see if the library already has a copy
of the requested book in its collection or if a copy of the
requested book is already on order from a publisher or
dealer.   The fourth step after searching is verification,
which means checking in some standard bibliographic
source to see if the book really exists and if the information about the book is correct.   Is the author's name in
correct form?   Is the title correct?   Who is the publisher
and when was the book published?   How much does the
book cost?   If there are any changes in the information
about the book in this step, the request must be searched
again.   The next step after verification is ordering.
Many libraries use multiple order forms to save typing
time.   Usually when the book is ordered from a publisher
or dealer, the Library of Congress catalog cards are
ordered from the Library of Congress.   The receipt of
the book is the next step.   At this point the books received
must be carefully checked with the books ordered to make
sure that the library has received the correct book and pos-
sibly the correct or desired edition of the book.   Also at this
point the multiple order forms are reunited with the book.
This means removing the copies of the order form which have
been filed in the order file or files of the library.

The next step is called cataloging.   The cataloger
must check to see if Library of Congress cards have been
ordered and if these printed cards have already arrived.
If the cards have been ordered but have not yet arrived the
cataloger must decide if temporary cataloging should be
done.   In some cases libraries simply allow the book to
wait for its printed LC cards.   If there are no LC cards
available for the book, then the cataloger must do original
cataloging indicating the author, the title, the edition, the
place of publication, the publisher, the date of publication,
the number of pages in the book, whether the book is
illustrated or not, the height of the book, and any other
pertinent information.   All of this information is included
on the catalog card as well as the call number and the
subject headings.   The call number consists of the classification number and the author number.   The subject headings are descriptive words or phrases indicating the subject content of the book.   The main card or unit card
must then be reproduced in as many copies as necessary.

The copies will have separate index entries typed at the top of each card for the subject headings and the title and any other basic index or access points.   The final step in processing the book consists of marking the call number on the spine of the book and including any necessary circulation materials in the book such as book cards, pockets, etc.   Any special binding will also be done at this stage. The final step for the card set for the book is the filing of the cards in the public catalog and the shelf list.

On the following pages the work of a technical services department is shown in flowchart form.   A flowchart is often used by librarians in this field because it distinguishes the sequence of procedures and, by different kinds of boxes, shows the type of operation involved and whether a decision or a process must be completed before the next step can be taken.   Each box has been labelled when first used for those who are not familiar with flowcharts.   In designing a procedure or in any analysis of an existing procedure a flowchart is especially useful because much information can be conveyed in very few words and symbols.

SUMMARY OF TECHNICAL PROCESSES

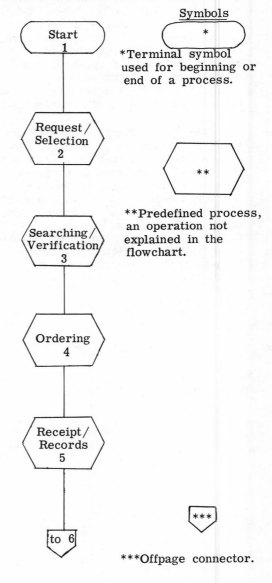

Symbols

*Terminal symbol used for beginning or end of a process.

**Predefined process, an operation not explained in the flowchart.

***Offpage connector.

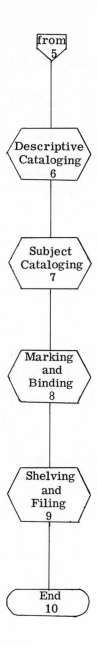

from
5

Descriptive
Cataloging
6

Subject
Cataloging
7

Marking
and
Binding
8

Shelving
and
Filing
9

End
10

11

REQUEST, SELECTION AND SEARCHING

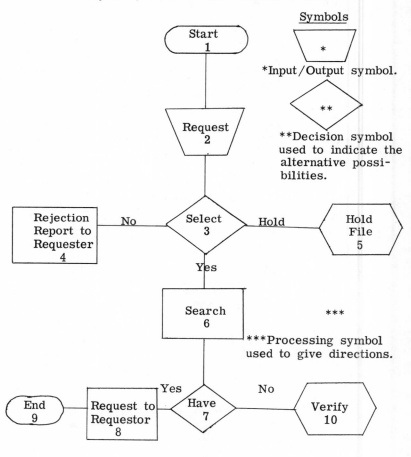

Symbols

*Input/Output symbol.

**Decision symbol used to indicate the alternative possibilities.

***Processing symbol used to give directions.

Start 1

Request 2

Rejection Report to Requester 4

No

Select 3

Hold

Hold File 5

Yes

Search 6

***

End 9

Request to Requestor 8

Yes

Have 7

No

Verify 10

12

VERIFICATION AND ORDERING

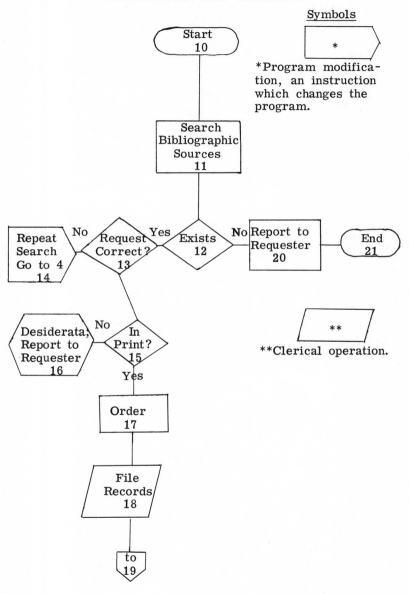

Symbols

*Program modification, an instruction which changes the program.

**Clerical operation.

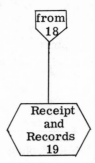

RECEIPT AND RECORDS

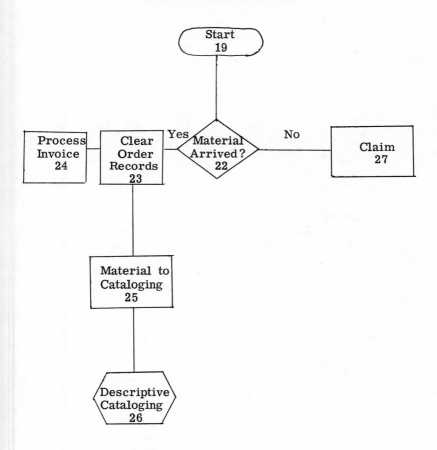

DESCRIPTIVE CATALOGING

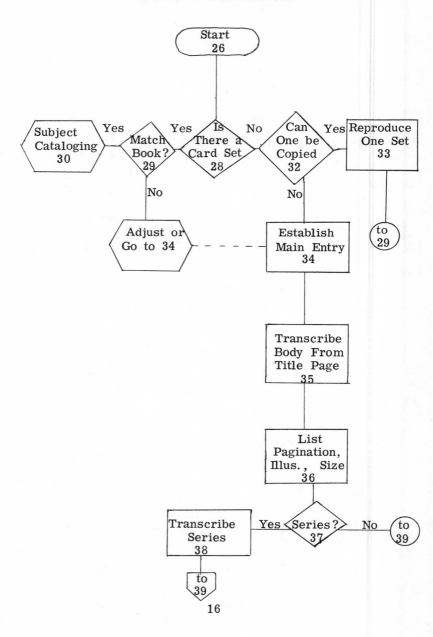

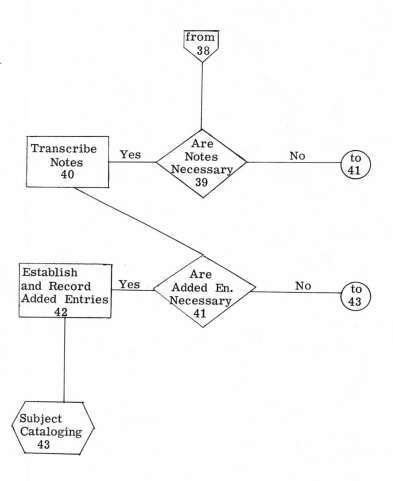

from
38

Transcribe
Notes
40

Yes

Are
Notes
Necessary
39

No

to
41

Establish
and Record
Added Entries
42

Yes

Are
Added En.
Necessary
41

No

to
43

Subject
Cataloging
43

SUBJECT CATALOGING

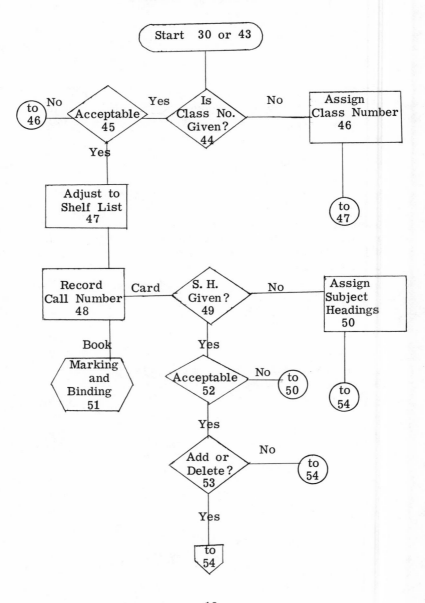

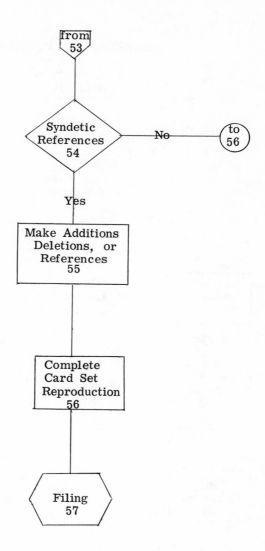

from
53

Syndetic
References
54

No → to 56

Yes

Make Additions
Deletions, or
References
55

Complete
Card Set
Reproduction
56

Filing
57

19

MARKING AND BINDING

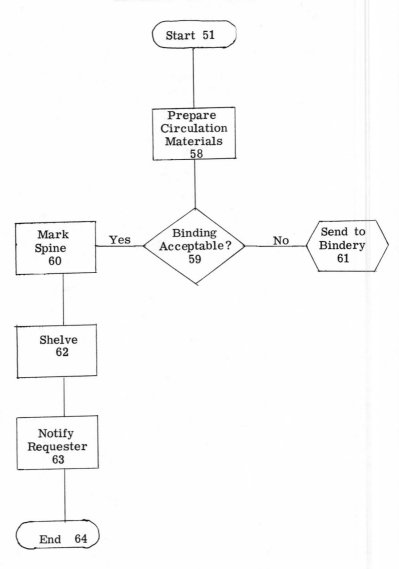

Start 51

Prepare
Circulation
Materials
58

Mark
Spine
60 — Yes — Binding
Acceptable?
59 — No — Send to
Bindery
61

Shelve
62

Notify
Requester
63

End   64

FILING THE CARDS

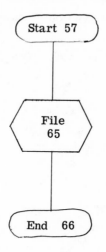

I. Introduction: Outline

A. <u>Definition and organization of technical services</u>

    1. Acquisitions

    2. Cataloging

    3. Serials

B. <u>Types of material</u>

    1. Books

        a. Monographs
        b. Serials
            (1) Periodicals
            (2) Non-periodicals
        c. Pamphlets

    2. Non-print materials

        a. Phonorecordings
        b. Film
        c. Machine readable data

    3. Manuscripts and Archives

    4. Artifacts

C. <u>Process of materials in technical services</u>

    1. Request and selection

    2. Searching and verification

    3. Ordering

    4. Receipt and records

5. Cataloging

    a. Ordering a card set
    b. Reproducing a card set
    c. Cards or other records show:
        (1) Author
        (2) Title
        (3) Subject content
    d. Completion of the card sets

6. Subject cataloging

    a. Assignment of a call number for location
    b. The subject classification
    c. Additional code for author, title, etc.
    d. Showing the subject content by subject
        headings
    e. Recording the call number in the book

7. Marking and binding

8. Shelving the book and filing the card set

PART 1: DESCRIPTIVE ANALYSIS

II. Bibliographic Description and Descriptive Cataloging

A. Introduction

Any bibliographic description will contain certain common elements such as the author and the title of the material being described. Bibliographic descriptions or citations may be found in bibliographies, footnotes, indexes, publishers' catalogs, and on library catalog cards. In order to prepare the necessary descriptive information for catalog cards it is necessary to identify and describe certain prescribed parts of books and other material. The basic elements of a bibliographic description of a book are the title, the edition, the place of publication, the publisher, the date of publication and/or copyright, the number of pages of the book, the type of illustrations, the height of the book, any necessary notes, and all possible entries including the author, the editor, any joint authors, and any other desired access points.

B. Bibliographic Description

Perhaps the most stable element of a bibliographic citation or description is the title or name of the material. The usual title for a book is found on the title-page and is called the title-page title. Also on the title-page may be a sub-title or second title in apposition with the title-page title. If this secondary title is introduced by the conjunction "or," catalogers call it an alternative title. The title of a book may also be found on the leaf preceding the title-page. If the title appears in this position it is called the half-title or bastard title. This form of the title may be identical with the title-page title or it may differ. The title on the front cover of a book is called the cover title while the title on the spine of a book is called the binder's title. In some books there is a title at the top of each page of the book. This form of the title is called the running title as it literally runs from page to page. Still another form of the title may be

found on the leaf preceding the text of the book. This title is
called the caption title. Any major variation which may be observed between the title-page title and any of these other forms
of the title should be noted in a bibliographic description.

The edition statement is another common element of
description. The edition of a book may be numbered such
as first, second, etc. or named such as revised, enlarged,
augmented, etc. Other identifying elements of an edition
may be the name of an editor, illustrator or translator.
Some books may also have a separate illustration statement
listing the type and/or number of illustrations. Directly
related to the edition statement is the name of the publisher, the date of publication and the place of publication.
These three elements are called the imprint. On the catalog card their order is always place, publisher and date.

A fourth characteristic feature of a bibliographic description is the collation. This is a physical description of
the book in terms of the number of pages or volumes, the type
of illustrations and the height of the book. Descriptions in publishers' catalogs would include the price of the book as part of
this description. The next element of the description includes
any significant notes or additional information about the book.
These include the name of any series of which the book is a
part, and if there are bibliographies in the book.

The last bibliographic characteristic of any book
deals with the authorship of the book. The author's name
is often the first element of a description such as it is on
the catalog card. For catalog cards there are strict rules
for the choice and form of an author's name. These rules
are covered in the following sections of this syllabus.

C.   Card Format

The first element on a unit card is the heading or main
entry. This is usually the verified form of the author's name.
The following section will discuss this in detail.

The second element on a unit card is called the
body of the card. The body consists of the title page
elements of the material. The first part of the body is
the title of the book or other material. This is followed
by any necessary repetition of the author statement as it

appears on the title page. The third element of the body is
the edition statement which may consist of the name and/or
number of an edition, the editor, the illustrator, the translator, etc. The last element of the body of the card is the imprint, consisting of the place of publication, the name of the
publisher, and the date of publication, in that order. If the
latest copyright date differs from the date of publication, both
are given. The four sections of the body of the card are consistent in that order. If any information necessary for one of
the four sections does not appear on the title page but, let us
say, on the page following the title page, that information will
be incorporated in the body of the card but placed in square
brackets to indicate that it does not appear on the title page.

The third part of the unit card is the collation, which is
the cataloger's physical description of the material. It consists of three parts: the pagination, the type of illustrations,
and the size. The pagination is recorded from the last numbered page of each numbering section of single volume works
and the total number of volumes for multi-volume works. The
type of illustrations may be simply cited as "illus." with only
maps receiving special indication. The size of the book is
measured in regard to the height of the book in centimeters
(a result of Melvil Dewey's interest in the metric system).
The order of the collation is also consistent.

The fourth section of the unit card is for notes about
the material. If a book is part of a series it may well have a
series note at the end of the collation line. All other notes
will appear as separate paragraphs below the collation.

The fifth section on a unit card is the tracing. This is
a record of the necessary supplementary entries that should
be produced to complete the card set. The subject headings
are listed in arabic numbers and the other added entries are
listed in Roman numerals. The prescribed order is:

    a. Heading: main entry
    b. Body
        (1) Title
        (2) Author Statement (if necessary)
        (3) Edition statement
            (a) Name and/or number
            (b) Editor
            (c) Illustrator, translator, etc.

Samples of Card Format

Call
no.
    HEADING
        BODY: Title, author, edition,
    imprint.
        COLLATION: pagination, illustrations,
    size.   SERIES NOTE.

    Descriptive Notes.

    TRACING.

    Tonne, Herbert Arthur, 1902-
        Methods of teaching business subjects
    [by] Herbert A. Tonne [and] Estelle L. Popham.
    3d ed.   New York, McGraw Hill [1965]
        vi, 488 p.   illus.   24 cm.

    Includes bibliographies.

        1.   BUSINESS EDUCATION.   I. Popham,
    Estelle L. , joint author.   II. Title.

      (4) Imprint
         (a) Place
         (b) Publisher
         (c) Date
  c. Collation
      (1) Pagination
      (2) Illustrations
      (3) Size
  d. Notes
      (1) Series statement at end of collation
      (2) Descriptive notes
      (3) Contents notes
  e. Tracing.

D. Descriptive Cataloging

According to the Anglo-American Cataloging Rules, the objectives of descriptive cataloging are:

> 1) to state the significant features of an item with the purpose of distinguishing it from other items and describing its scope, contents, and bibliographic relation to other items; 2) to present these data in an entry which can be integrated with the entries for other items in the catalog and which will respond best to the interests of most users of the catalog.

This section deals with the necessary rules for the descriptive cataloging of separately published monographs. Both the 1949 Library of Congress Rules for Descriptive Cataloging and the new Anglo-American Cataloging Rules (AAC) have been carefully studied and incorporated when appropriate.

The process of descriptive cataloging, as the following rules demonstrate, consists of describing and identifying each separate bibliographical unit in a collection. The rules for separately published monographs deal with rules governing the body of entry, the collation, and the series statement. The body of the entry consists of the title statement, the author statement, the edition statement, and the imprint, as has been previously stated. The collation consists of the pagination or number of volumes, the type of illustrative matter, and the height of the book. The series statement represents a statement that a book is a part of a particular series.

As the new code (the AAC) does not represent any major changes from the 1949 LC <u>Rules</u>, there are very few problems similar to some of the changes in authorship rules. It should be noted that since 1964 the author statement has been generally included in the body of the card. Also it should be noted that the rules for informal notes have been largely rearranged from the former rules.

II. Bibliographic Description and Descriptive Cataloging: Outline

A. Introduction and definitions

B. Bibliographic Description

    1. Various forms of the title

        a. Title-page title
        b. Sub-title
        c. Alternative title
        d. Cover title
        e. Binder's title
        f. Half-title
        g. Running title
        h. Caption title

    2. Edition

        a. Edition number
        b. Edition statement
        c. Editor
        d. Illustrator, translator

    3. Imprint

        a. Place of publication
        b. Publisher's name
        c. Date of publication, copyright date

    4. Collation

        a. Pagination or number of volumes
        b. Type of illustrations
        c. Size

    5. Notes

        a. Series' name

        b.   Descriptive notes
        c.   Contents notes

   6.   Possible entries

        a.   Author
        b.   Editor
        c.   Title
        d.   Other

C.   <u>Card Format</u>

   1.   Heading

   2.   Body

        a.   Title
        b.   Author Statement
        c.   Edition Statement
            (1)   Name and/or Number
            (2)   Editor
            (3)   Illustrator, Translator, etc.
        d.   Imprint
            (1)   Place
            (2)   Publisher
            (3)   Date

   3.   Collation

        a.   Pagination
        b.   Type of Illustration
        c.   Size

   4.   Notes

        a.   Series Statement at end of Collation
        b.   Descriptive Notes
        c.   Contents Notes

   5.   Tracing

D.   <u>Introduction to Descriptive Cataloging</u>

   1.   Definition

   2.   Principles

3. Purpose

    a. Identification
    b. Description

4. Organization of the description (AAC 130)

5. Source of the description (AAC 131)

E. Rules governing the body of the entry

    1. Relationship of the title page to the description of a work (AAC 132)

    2. The recording of the title (AAC 137)

    3. The author statement (AAC 134)

    4. The edition statement (AAC 135)

    5. The illustration statement (AAC 135)

    6. The imprint statement (AAC 138)

        a. Place of publication (AAC 139)
        b. Publisher (AAC 140)
        c. Date (AAC 141)

F. Rules covering the collation

    1. Pagination (AAC 142A & 142B)

    2. Illustrative matter (AAC 142C)

    3. Size (AAC 142D)

G. Introduction to notes (AAC 144A-D)

    1. Informal notes

    2. Conventional notes

        a. Series statement (AAC 143)
        b. "At head of title" note (AAC 145)
        c. Bibliographies (AAC 149A4 & 149C7)

H. Tracing of secondary entries (AAC 151)

II. Bibliographic Description and Descriptive Cataloging: Readings

Basic Readings

Anglo-American Cataloging Rules, Prepared by the American Library Association, the Library of Congress, the Library Association, and the Canadian Library Association. North American Text. Chicago: American Library Association, 1967.
Pp. 189-225. British text, pp. 161-179.

Wynar, Bohdan S. Introduction to Cataloging and Classification. 3d ed. Rochester, N.Y.: Libraries Unlimited, 1967.
Pp. 24-33; 110-131.

Enrichment Readings

Bidlack, Russell E. Typewritten Catalog Cards, A Manual of Procedure and Form with 125 Sample Cards. Ann Arbor, Mich.: Ann Arbor Publishers, c1959.

Cataloging Rules of the American Library Association and the Library of Congress: Additions and Changes, 1949-58. Washington: The Library of Congress, 1959.
Pp. 59-76.

Colvin, Laura C. Cataloging Sampler, a Comparative and Interpretive Guide. Hamden, Conn.: The Shoe String Press, 1963.

Jolley, Leonard. The Principles of Cataloguing. New York: Philosophical Library, 1961.
Pp. 126-139.

U.S. Library of Congress. Rules for Descriptive Cataloging. Washington: Govt. Print. Off., 1949.

II. Bibliographic Description and Descriptive Cataloging

Samples of Catalog Cards

AAC 132 A1   RELATIONSHIP OF THE TITLE PAGE
              TO THE DESCRIPTION OF A WORK

Use of brackets for additional data:

Chicago. Art Institute.
Ivan Albright; a retrospective exhibition organized by the
Art Institute of Chicago in collaboration with the Whitney
Museum of American Art. The Art Institute of Chicago:
October 30–December 27, 1964; the Whitney Museum of
American Art: February 3–March 21, 1965. Catalogue by
Frederick A. Sweet with a commentary by Jean Dubuffet.
₁Chicago ʔ 1964₁

Balcer, Charles Lewis, 1921–
Teaching speech in today's secondary schools ₁by₁ Charles
L. Balcer ₁and₁ Hugh F. Seabury. New York, Holt, Rine-
hart and Winston ₁1965₁

x, 435 p.   24 cm.

Includes bibliographies.

Berkhofer, Robert F
Salvation and the savage; an analysis of Protestant mis-
sions and American Indian response, 1787–1862. ₁Lexing-
ton₁ University of Kentucky Press ₁1965₁

xiv, 186 p.   23 cm.

"Bibliographical essay": p. ₁161₁–180.

Meiklejohn, Donald.
Freedom and the public; public and private morality in
America. ₁1st ed. Syracuse, N. Y.₁ Syracuse University
Press ₁1965₁

ix, 163 p.   22 cm.

Bibliographical references included in "Notes to chapters" (p. 155–
160)

1. Citizenship—U. S.   2. Political ethics.   3. Liberty.   4. Political
science—Hist.—U. S.   ɪ. Title.

JK1768.M4   323.60973   65—23650

Library of Congress   ₁65₅₁

U. S. *Library of Congress. Processing dept.*
... Filing manual. Washington, 1945–

1 v. 27 cm.

Cover-title.
Loose-leaf.

1. Alphabeting. ɪ. Title. 2. Indexing. 3. Files
and filing (Documents).
Z696.U57   025.3   45—35965

Library of Congress   ₍53d1₎

₍Defoe, Daniel₎ 1661–1731.
The history of the devil, ancient and modern. In two parts
... In which is included, a description of the devil's dwelling
... London, G. Hay, 1777.

viii, 340 p. 16ᶜᵐ.

Brett, George Sidney, 1879–1944.
Brett's History of psychology. Edited and abridged by
R. S. Peters. ₍2d rev. ed.₎ Cambridge, Mass., M. I. T.
Press ₍1965₎

778 p. 21 cm. (The M. I. T. paperback series, MIT24)

Bibliography : p. ₍769₎–772.

Johnson, Alexander Bryan, 1786–1867.
Alexander Bryan Johnson's A treatise on language, ed.,
with a critical essay on his philosophy of language, by David
Rynin. Berkeley, Univ. of California Press, 1947.

ix, 443 p. port., facsims. 24 cm.

"A treatise on language: ... first published in 1836, is itself an ex-
panded and revised edition of Johnson's earlier work, The philosophy
of human knowledge, published in 1828, based on lectures delivered in
Utica in 1825."—p. vii.
"A critical essay on Johnson's philosophy of language": p. 305–430.
"Corriegenda": leaf inserted.

1. Language and languages. ɪ. Rynin, David, 1905– ed.

P103.J66   1947   401   47—30311*

Library of Congress   ₍62u¾₎

AAC 133 E   ADDITIONS TO THE TITLE

Weiss, Peter, 1916–
   The persecution and assassination of Jean-Paul Marat
as performed by the inmates of the Asylum of Charenton
under the direction of the Marquis de Sade; ₍a play₎ English version by Geoffrey Skelton.   Verse adaptation by
Adrian Mitchell. Introd. by Peter Brook. ₍1st American
ed.₎ New York, Atheneum ₍1966, °1965₎

   x, 117 p. 22 cm.

   Includes music.

   1. Marat, Jean Paul, 1743–1793—Drama.   ɪ. Title.

   PT2685.E5V43   1966   832.914   65—15915

   Library of Congress   ₍a67k7₎

AAC 132 C   ALTERNATIVE TITLE

Kirkpatrick, Thomas Winfrid, 1896–
   Better English for technical authors; or,
Call a spade a spade, by T. W. Kirkpatrick
and M. H. Breese.   New York, Macmillan,
1961.
   122p. illus. 23 cm.

   I. Breese, M. J., joint author.   II. Title.
III. Title: Call a spade a spade.

AAC 134 A   AUTHOR STATEMENT

Kerenskiĭ, Aleksandr Fedorovich, 1881–
    Russia and history's turning point, by Alexander Keren-
sky. ₁1st ed.₎ New York, Duell, Sloan and Pearce ₁1965₎
    xvi, 558 p. illus., ports. 24 cm.

Freeman, Barbara Constance.
    Broom-Adelaide, written and illustrated by Barbara C.
Freeman. ₁1st American ed.₎ Boston, Little, Brown ₁1965₎
    124 p. illus. 22 cm.

    "An Atlantic Monthly Press book."

Knights, Lionel Charles, 1906–
    Further explorations, by L. C. Knights. Stanford, Calif.,
Stanford University Press, 1965.
    203 p. 23 cm.

    Essays.
    Bibliographical footnotes.

    1. Shakespeare, William, 1564–1616—Criticism and interpretation.
2. English literature—Addresses, essays, lectures. ɪ. Title.

PR2976.K639 1965   o2.33   65–16859

Library of Congress   ₁5₎

AAC 134 A   AUTHOR STATEMENT (cont'd.)

Bohner. Charles H
    Robert Penn Warren, by Charles H. Bohner. New York,
Twayne Publishers ₁1965, ᶜ1964₁
     175 p.   21 cm.   (Twayne's United States authors series, 69)
     Bibliography: p. 166–168.

Winner, Thomas Gustav, 1917–
    Chekhov and his prose, by Thomas Winner. ₁1st ed.₁
New York, Holt. Rinehart and Winston ₁1966₁
     xviii, 263 p.   21 cm.
     Bibliographical references included in "Notes" (p. 245–251)

Wright, Andrew H
    Henry Fielding, mask and feast, by Andrew Wright.
Berkeley, University of California Press, 1965.
     213 p.   23 cm.
     Bibliographical references included in "Notes": p. 193–208.

     1. Fielding, Henry, 1707–1754.

PR3457.W7   823.5   65—1968

     Library of Congress   ₁65c2₁

AAC 134 D   JOINT AUTHORS

> **Boyd, Jessie Edna,** 1899–
> Books, libraries and you; a handbook on the use of refer-
> ence books and the reference resources of the library ₍by₎
> Jessie Boyd ₍and others₎ 3d ed. New York, Scribner ₍1965₎
>
> xii, 205 p. illus. 22 cm.
>
>
>
> 1. Libraries and readers. 2. **Reference books.** 3. **Reference**
> books—Bibl.   i. Title.
>
> Z711.2.B7 1965   028.7   65—12298
>
> Library of Congress   ₍66f14₎

AAC 134 E   OMISSIONS FROM THE AUTHOR
STATEMENT

> **Frazer,** *Sir* **James George,** 1854–1941.
> Aftermath; a supplement to The golden bough, by Sir
> James George Frazer ... London, Macmillan and co., lim-
> ited, 1936.
>
> xx, 404 p. 23 cm.

> **Oliphant, Margaret Oliphant (Wilson)** 1828–1897.
> The makers of Florence; Dante, Giotto, Savonarola, and
> their city, by Mrs. Oliphant ... With portrait of Savonarola
> engraved by C. H. Jeens and illustrations from drawings by
> Professor Delamotte. London, Macmillan & co., limited;
> New York, The Macmillan company, 1897.
>
> xx, 422 p. incl. front. (port.) illus., plates. 19 cm.
>
> First published 1876.
>
> 1. Florence—Hist. 2. Dante Alighieri, 1265–1321. 3. Giotto di
> Bondone, 1266?–1337. 4. Savonarola, Girolamo Maria Francesco
> Matteo, 1452–1498.   i. Title.
>
> DG737.O47   2—2523
>
> Library of Congress   ₍58i²2₎

Hart, James David, 1911–
  The Oxford companion to American literature ₍by₎ James
D. Hart. 4th ed. ₍rev. and enl.₎ New York, Oxford Uni-
versity Press, 1965.

  ix, 991 p. 25 cm.

  1. American literature—Dictionaries.   2. American literature—
Bio-bibl.   ɪ. Title.

  PS21.H3 1965   810.3   65—22796

  Library of Congress   ₍a67p³7₎

Silverberg, Robert.
  Scientists and scoundrels; a book of hoaxes. Illustrated
by Jerome Snyder. New York, Crowell ₍1965₎

  x, 251 p. illus. 21 cm.

  Bibliography: p. 239–245.

Price, Christine, 1928–
  Cities of gold and isles of spice; travel to the East in the
Middle Ages. Maps and decorations by the author. New
York, D. McKay Co., 1965.

  xiii, 208 p. illus., maps. 21 cm.

Catlin, George, 1796–1872.
  Letters and notes on the manners, customs, and condition
of the North American Indians, written during eight years'
travel amongst the wildest tribes of Indians in North America in 1832, 33, 34, 35, 36, 37, 38, and 39. With 400 illus.,
carefully engr. from his original paintings. Minneapolis,
Ross & Haines, 1965.

  2 v. illus., maps, ports. 25 cm.

  "First issued 1841."

  1. Indians of North America. 2. Indians of North America—The
West.   ɪ. Title.

  E77.C38 1965   970.1   65–2468

  Library of Congress   ₍3₎   .

Boyden, David Dodge, 1910–
The history of violin playing, from its origins to 1761 and its relationship to the violin and violin music ₍by₎ David D. Boyden.   London, New York, Oxford University Press, 1965.

xxiii, 569 p.   illus., facsims., map, music, ports.   26 cm.

Langwill, Lyndesay Graham, 1897–
The bassoon and contrabassoon ₍by₎ Lyndesay G. Langwill.   London, E. Benn; New York, W. W. Norton ₍1965₎

xiv, 269 p.   illus., facsims., music.   23 cm.   (Instruments of the orchestra)

Wuorinen, John Henry, 1897–
A history of Finland, by John H. Wuorinen.   New York, Published for American-Scandinavian Foundation by Columbia University Press, 1965.

xv, 548 p.   illus., maps, ports.   24 cm.

Bibliography : p. ₍529₎–535.

1. Finland—Hist.   ɪ. Title.

DK451.W8   947.1   65—13618

Library of Congress   ₍66f4₎

Bradley, John Grover, 1886–
A national film library; the problem of selection.   ₍Presented Oct. 15, 1945, at the Technical Conference in New York.   n. p., ᶜ1946₎

64–72 p.   23 cm.

Caption title.
"Reprinted from the Journal of the Society of Motion Picture Engineers, vol. 47, no. 1, July 1946."

1. U. S. Library of Congress. Motion Picture Division.
ɪ. Title.

Z733.U63M52   025.177   51—62782

Library of Congress   ₍1₎

Steers, James Alfred, 1899–
The coastline of England and Wales, by J. A. Steers. [2d
ed. Cambridge [Eng.] University Press, 1964.

xxviii, 750 p. illus., maps (part fold.)   24 cm.

Slusher, Howard S   *ed.*
Anthology of contemporary readings; an introduction to
physical education [by] Howard S. Slusher [and] Aileene
S. Lockhart. Dubuque, Iowa, W. C. Brown Co. [1966]

ix, 324 p. illus. 24 cm. (Brown physical education series)

Includes bibliographies.

1. Physical education and training — Addresses, essays, lectures.
I. Lockhart, Aileene Simpson, 1911–   joint ed. II. Title.

GV361.S55   613.7   66—14912

Library of Congress   [66f5]

Marceau, LeRoy.
Drafting a union contract. Edited by Raymond E. Bjork-
back. Boston, Little, Brown, 1965.

xxix, 321 p. 24 cm.

American Paper and Pulp Association.
The dictionary of paper, including pulp, paperboard,
paper properties, and related papermaking terms. 3d ed.
New York, 1965.

xii, 500 p. 24 cm.

Bibliography : p. 487–489.

1. Paper—Dictionaries. 2. Paper making and trade—Dictionaries.

TS1085.A6 1965   676.03   65–2940

Library of Congress   [2]

AAC 141   DATE

Nordenskjöld, Otto, 1869–1928.
    The geography of the polar regions, consisting of a general characterization of polar nature, by Otto Nordenskjöld, and, a regional geography of the Arctic and the Antarctic, by Ludwig Mecking. New York, American Geographical Society, 1928 ₍i. e. 1950₎

vi, 359 p. illus., maps. 24 cm. (American Geographical Society of New York. Special publication no. 8)

North Dakota. *Laws, statutes, etc.*
    North Dakota century code; comprising statutes of a general and permanent nature including those enacted by the Thirty-sixth Legislative Assembly. Published by authority of the Legislative Assembly under the supervision of the Legislative Research Committee and the Secretary of State. Indianapolis, A. Smith Co. ₍1959–60₎

14 v. 26 cm.

Akademiíà nauk SSSR. *Institut ėkonomiki.*
    Political economy, a textbook. Moscow, State Pub. House of Political Literature, 1954. ₍n. p., 1955 ?₎

401 p. 27 cm.

Swinton, William, 1833–1892.
    Outlines of the world's history, ancient, mediæval, and modern, with special relation to the history of civilization and the progress of mankind ... ₍Rev. ed.₎ By William Swinton ... New York, Cincinnati ₍etc.₎ American book company ₍187– ?₎

xi, ₍1₎, 498 p. illus., 6 double maps. 17½ᶜᵐ.

First edition, 1874.

1. History, Universal.

17—20698

Library of Congress   D21.S97   1874 a

₍a41b1₎

Fisher, Dorothea Frances (Canfield) 1879–1958.
The Montessori manual for teachers and parents. Cambridge, Mass., R. Bentley, 1964 [°1913]

126 p. illus. (1 col.) port. 22 cm.

Jones, Genesius.
Approach to the purpose; a study of the poetry of T. S.
Eliot. New York, Barnes & Noble [1965, °1964]

351 p. 23 cm.

"List of works consulted": p. 342–346.

Delgado, Alan.
Introducing ponies. London, Spring Books [n. d.]

unpaged. illus. 29 cm.

1. Ponies. 2. Horses—Pictures, illustrations, etc.

[SF315]   636.16084   61–19924 ‡

Printed for Alanar
by Library of Congress   [2]

Pearl, Richard Maxwell, 1913–
Colorado gem trails and mineral guide [by] Richard M.
Pearl. Sketch maps by Mignon Wardell Pearl. 2d rev. ed.
Denver, Sage Books [1965]

223 p. illus., maps. 23 cm.

Includes bibliographies.

1. Mineralogy—Colorado. 2. Precious stones—Colorado.
3. Precious stones—Collectors and collecting. I. Title.

QE375.C6P4 1965   549.9788   65–16515

Library of Congress   [5]

AAC 142   COLLATION (cont'd.)

Selsam, Millicent (Ellis) 1912–
    Let's get turtles, by Millicent E. Selsam.   Drawings by
Arnold Lobel.   New York, Harper & Row ₁1965₁

    62 l.   col. illus.   22 cm.   (A Science I can read book)

Encyclopædia Britannica.
    Encyclopædia Britannica world atlas; world distributions
and world political geography, political-physical maps,
geographical summaries, geographical comparisons, glossary
of geographical terms, index to political-physical maps.   G.
Donald Hudson, geographical editor.   Under the general
editorial direction of Walter Yust.   Unabridged.   Chicago
₁1955₁

    xii, ₁63₁, 117, iv, 384 p.   illus., maps (part col.)   38 cm.

Peach, John Vincent, 1936–
    Cosmology and Christianity, by J. V. Peach.   ₁1st ed.₁
New York, Hawthorn Books ₁1965₁

    107 ₁3₁ p.   illus.   21 cm.   (The Twentieth century encyclopedia of
Catholicism, v. 127.   Section 13 : Catholicism and science)

    Bibliography : p. ₁110₁

Wilcox, Ruth Turner, 1888–
    Folk and festival costume of the world ₁by₁ R. Turner
Wilcox.   New York, Scribner ₁1965₁

    1 v. (unpaged)   illus.   28 cm.

    Includes bibliography.

    1. Costume.   I. Title.

    GT510.W54   391   65–23986

    Library of Congress   ₁5₁

AAC 142   COLLATION (cont'd.)

Family Service Association of America. *Midwestern Regional Committee. Committee on Family Diagnosis and Treatment.*
    Casebook on family diagnosis and treatment; seven cases from family agency practice with an introduction containing theories and concepts and a case reading guide. Selected and prepared by the Committee on Family Diagnosis and Treatment of the Midwestern Regional Committee, Family Service Association of America. New York, Family Service Association of America, 1965.
    1 v. (various pagings)   28 cm.
    1. Social case work.   2. Family.   I. Title.

Illinois. University. *Committee on School Mathematics.*
    High school mathematics. Units 1 through 4.   Teachers' ed. Urbana, University of Illinois Press, 1959.
    4 v.   illus.   30 cm.

Young, Ione (Dodson)
    A concordance to the poetry of Byron.   Austin, Tex., Pemberton Press, 1965.
    4 v. (xv,1698 p.)   28 cm.

    1. Byron, George Gordon Noël Byron, baron, 1788–1824.   I. Title.

PR4395.Y6   821.7   66—674

Library of Congress   [66b1]

AAC 142 C   ILLUSTRATIVE MATTER

Johnston, Johanna.
> Together in America; the story of two races and one nation. Illustrated by Mort Künstler. New York, Dodd, Mead [1965]
>> 158 p. illus. 24 cm.

Wildsmith, Brian.
> Brian Wildsmith's 1, 2, 3's. New York, F. Watts, 1965.
>> 1 v. (chiefly col. illus.) 29 cm.

1. Numeration—Juvenile literature.   i. Title: 1, 2, 3's.

PZ10.W65Br   **J** 511   65–10782

Library of Congress   [3]

AAC 142 D   SIZE

Soyinka, Wole.
> The road; [a play] London, Oxford University Press, 1965.
>> 101 p. 19 cm. (A Three crowns book)

Sendak, Maurice.
> Hector Protector, and As I went over the water; two nursery rhymes with pictures. New York, Harper & Row [1965]
>> 1 v. (unpaged) col. illus. 19 x 22 cm.

i. Title. ii. Title: As I went over the water.

PZ8.3.S4684He   65–8256

Library of Congress   [4–1]

Gould, Samuel B
  The library: core of conscience and community [by] Samuel B. Gould. Geneseo, N. Y., State University College, 1965.

  16 p. port. 22 cm. (Mary C. Richardson lecture, 8th)

Astrinsky, Aviva.
  A bibliography of South African English novels, 1930–1960. [Cape Town] University of Cape Town, School of Librarianship, 1965.

  57 p. 23 cm. (University of Cape Town. School of Librarianship. Bibliographical series)

  1. English fiction—South African authors—Bibl. 2. South African fiction (English)—Bibl. I. Title. (Series: Cape Town. University of Cape Town. School of Librarianship. Bibliographical series)

Li, Shu-t'ien, 1900–
  Chronological and classified bibliography on prestressed concrete piling and associated technology, 1946–1966. [Rapid City, S. D.] 1966.

  viii, 70 l. 28 cm. (*His* Monographs on prestressed concrete piling technology, 10)

  1. Concrete piling—Bibl. 2. Prestressed concrete construction—Bibl. I. Title.

British Geomorphological Research Group.
  A bibliography of British geomorphology. Compiled by members of the British Geomorphological Research Group. Edited by Keith M. Clayton. London, G. Philip [1964]

  x, 211 p. 22 cm. (*Its* Occasional paper no. 1)

  1. Geomorphology—Gt. Brit.—Bibl. I. Clayton, Keith M., ed. II. Title. (Series)

  Z6004.P5B68   66–93754

  Library of Congress   [2]

AAC 144 E   INFORMAL NOTES

U. S. *Library of Congress. Processing dept.*
... Filing manual. Washington, 1945–

1 v. 27 cm.

Cover-title.
Loose-leaf.

Commerce Clearing House.
Dictionary of labor law terms. 2d ed. Chicago, 1953.

144 p. 16 cm.

On cover : CCH labor law reports edition.

Jarrell, Randall, 1914–
The lost world. ₁1st ed.₁ New York, Macmillan ₁ᶜ1965₁

69 p. 22 cm.

Poems.

Political and Economic Planning.
New Commonwealth students in Britain, with special reference to students from East Africa. London, Allen & Unwin ₁1965₁

253 p. 23 cm.

Label stamped on t. p.: Distributed by Sportshelf, New Rochelle,
N. Y.
"Written by Jean Currie and Timothy Leggatt."
Companion to Education for a developing region, by Guy Hunter.

1. Education—Africa, East. 2. African students in Gt. Brit.
I. Currie, Jean. II. Leggatt, Timothy. III. Title.

LA1561.P6   65–6193

Library of Congress   ₁3₁

AAC 144 E   INFORMAL NOTES (cont'd.)

Trofskiĭ, Lev, 1879–1940.
    The Trotsky papers, 1917–1922. Edited and annotated by
Jan M. Meijer. The Hague, Mouton, 1964–
        v. (Internationaal Instituut voor Sociale Geschiedenis. Russian
series)
        Russian and English.
        Includes correspondence between Lenin and Trotsky.
        Bibliography: v. 1, p. 827–834. Bibliographical footnotes.

Godfrey, Frederick M
    History of Italian painting, 1250–1800 [by] F. M. God-
frey. New York, Taplinger Pub. Co. [1965]
        xii, 456 p. illus., map, 12 col. plates. 23 cm.

        Second ed., rev. and enl., of the author's A student's guide to early
Italian painting, 1250–1500 and A student's guide to later Italian
painting, 1500–1800.
        Bibliography: p. 427–429.

Freedman, Leonard, *ed.*
    Issues of the sixties; second edition, 1965–1970. Belmont,
Calif., Wadsworth Pub. Co. [1965]
        x, 414 p. 23 cm. (Wadsworth continuing education series)

        Not a revision of the work of the same title published in 1961 but
a new set of readings.

Jackson, Brian.
    Streaming: an education system in miniature. London,
Routledge & K. Paul [1964]
        ix, 156 p. 23 cm. (Reports of the Institute of Community Studies,
11)
        Label mounted on t. p.: New York, Humanities Press.
        Bibliography: p. 152–154.

        1. Ability grouping in education. 2. Education, Elementary. 3.
Education—Gt. Brit.   ɪ. Title.   (Series: Institute of Community
Studies. Report, 11)

LB3061.J3   371.25   65–3016

Library of Congress   [2]

AAC 144 E   INFORMAL NOTES (cont'd.)

Anderson, George William, *ed.*   A new, authentic, and
complete collection of voyages round the world ...   (Card 2)

mediate direction of George William Anderson, Esq., assisted by a principal officer and by other gentlemen of the
Royal Navy. London, Printed for A. Hogg ₁17—₁

826+ p. plates, port., charts. 39 cm.

L. C. copy imperfect: all after p. 826 wanting.
Binder's title: Voyages of Cap'n James Cook.

Wilde, Oscar, 1854–1900.
... The works of Oscar Wilde ... with an introduction by
Richard Le Gallienne ... New York, Lamb publishing co.,
1909.

15 v. fronts., plates, ports. 21 cm. (Sunflower edition)
"The Sunflower edition is limited to one thousand ... copies, of
which this is no. 556."
The illustrations are on Japan paper.
CONTENTS.
₁I₁ Poems.
₁II₁ Dorian Gray.
₁III₁ House of pomegranates: The young king; The birthday of the
infanta; The fisherman and his soul; The star-child. The happy
prince. The nightingale and the rose. The selfish giant. The devoted friend. The remarkable rocket.

Albers, Henry Herman, 1919–
Principles of organization and management ₁by₁ Henry
H. Albers. 2d ed. New York, J. Wiley ₁1965₁

xii, 676 p. 24 cm.

Previously published under title: Organized executive action.
Includes bibliographical references.

Wilson, John Anthony Burgess, 1917–
Re Joyce ₁by₁ Anthony Burgess. New York, W. W.
Norton ₁1965₁

272 p. 22 cm.

London ed. (Faber) has title: Here comes everybody.

1. Joyce, James, 1882–1941.   I. Title.

PR6019.O9Z96 1965   823.912   65—18779

Library of Congress   ₁67d7₁

AAC 144 E   INFORMAL NOTES (cont'd.)

Montessori, Maria, 1870–1952.
    The Montessori method; scientific pedagogy as applied to
child education in "the Children's Houses" with additions
and revisions by the author. Translated from the Italian
by Anne E. George. With an introd. by Martin Mayer.
Cambridge, Mass., R. Bentley, 1965.
    xli. 386 p. illus., forms, ports. 22 cm.
    Translation of Il metodo della pedagogia scientifica.
    Originally published in 1912; reissued in 1964.

Shestov, Lev, 1866–1938.
    Chekhov, and other essays.   New introd. by Sidney Monas.
ₜAnn Arborₗ University of Michigan Press ₜ1966ₗ
    xxvi, 205 p. 21 cm. (Ann Arbor paperbacks, AA113)
    Translation of Начала и концы (transliterated: Nachala i kont͡sy)

Jednota československých matematiků a fysiků v Praze.
    Études phonologiques dédiées à la mémoire de M. le Prince
N. S. Trubetzkoy. Pref. by Carroll E. Reed. University,
University of Alabama Press ₜ1964ₗ
    345 p. 21 cm. (Alabama linguistic and philological series, #2)
    "Originally published in 1939 in Prague by Jednota českých mate-
matiků a fysiků as #8 of the Travaux du cercle linguistique de
Prague."
    French or English.
    Includes bibliographical references.

Council of Europe. *Council for Cultural Co-operation.*
    Bibliographie d'ouvrages sur l'Europe, à l'intention des
enseignants. Strasbourg, Conseil de l'Europe, 1965.
    68 p. 20 cm. unpriced
                                (F 66–7257)
    At head of title: Conseil de la coopération culturelle du Conseil de
l'Europe.
    Issued also under title: Books dealing with Europe.

    1. Europe—Bibl.   ɪ. Title.

Z2000.C6314   016.914   66–66669

Library of Congress   ₜ2ₗ

AAC 144 E   INFORMAL NOTES (cont'd.)

Johnson, Stanley P   1892–1946.
The complete reporter; a general text in journalistic writing and editing, complete with exercises [by] Julian Harriss
and Stanley Johnson. 2d ed.   New York, Macmillan [1965]

viii, 472 p.   illus.   22 cm.

In the earlier ed. Johnson's name appeared first on the title
page.
Bibliography: p. 464–467.

Haugaard, Erik Christian.
A slave's tale.   Illustrated by Leo and Diane Dillon.   Boston, Houghton Mifflin, 1965.

217 p.   illus.   22 cm.

Sequel to Hakon of Rogen's saga.

Proust, Marcel, 1871–1922.
Within a budding grove, by Marcel Proust, translated by
C. K. Scott Moncrieff ...   New York, The Modern library
[1930]

5 p. l., 356 p.   17 cm.   (*Half-title:* The Modern library of the
world's best books)

" 'Within a budding grove' is the second novel in Proust's life work,
'Remembrance of things past.' "
"First Modern library edition 1930."

Conybeare, John Josias, 1779–1824.
Illustrations of Anglo-Saxon poetry.   Edited, together
with additional notes, introductory notices, &c., by William
Daniel Conybeare.   New York, Haskell House, 1964.

xcvi, 286 p.   24 cm.

Reprint of work first published in 1826.

1. Anglo-Saxon poetry.   2. Anglo-Saxon poetry—Translations.   3.
Anglo-Saxon language—Versification.   4. Anglo-Saxon poetry—Bibl.
I. Conybeare, William Daniel, 1787–1857, ed.   II. Title.

PR1505.C63   1964   65–15875

Library of Congress   [18–1]

AAC 144 E   INFORMAL NOTES (cont'd.)

Lawler, Lillian Beatrice, 1898–
   The dance in ancient Greece, by Lillian B. Lawler. ₁1st
American ed.₁ Middletown, Conn., Wesleyan University
Press ₁1965, °1964₁

   160 p.   62 illus.   23 cm.

   "Much of the material in the book appeared first in 1962, in the
form of an issue of Dance perspectives, under the title Terpsichore:
the story of the dance in ancient Greece."
   Bibliographical references included in "Notes" (p. 145–154)

Rich, Barnabe, 1540?–1617.
   Faultes, faults, and nothing else but faultes (1606) by
Barnaby Rich. A facsimile reproduction. Edited with
introd. and notes by Melvin H. Wolf. Gainesville, Fla.,
Scholars' Facsimiles & Reprints, 1965.

   263 p.   23 cm.

   "Reproduced from a copy in ... Henry E. Huntington Library."
   Bibliography: p. 255–263.

   1. Conduct of life—Quotations, maxims, etc.   ɪ. Title.

   PR2336.R8F34   1606a   827.3   65–10396

   Library of Congress   ₁5₁

AAC 145   "AT HEAD OF TITLE" NOTE

Rand Corporation.
   Selected list of unclassified research memoranda of the
Economics Division of the Rand Corporation ₁by the₁ Eco-
nomics Division. Rev. Santa Monica, Calif., 1957.

   16 l.   29 cm.   (*Its* Research memorandum, RM–821–5)

   At head of title: U. S. Air Force, Project Rand.
   "ASTIA document number AD144281."

   1. Economics—Bibl.   2. Russia—Econ. condit.—Bibl.   (Series)

   Q180.A1R36   no. 821   016.330947   58—33056

   Library of Congress   ₁60b1₁

Higgins, Richard Carter.
  Jefferson's birthday, by Dick Higgins. New York, Something Else Press [1964]
  x, 271 p. illus. 21 cm.
  Bound with the author's Postface. New York [1964]

Higgins, Richard Carter.
  Postface, by Dick Higgins. New York, Something Else Press [1964]
  90 p. illus. 21 cm.
  Bound with the author's Jefferson's birthday. New York [1964]
  Bibliographical references included in "Footnotes" (p. 89)

  i. Title.

  PS3558.I 36J4   709.04   65–706

  Library of Congress   [2]

Ludovico degli Arrighi, *Vicentino*, *fl.* 1522.
  Il modo de temperare le penne con le uarie sorti de littere ordinato per Ludouico Vicentino. Roma, 1523.
  [31] p. 21 cm.
  Bound with the author's La operina. [Roma, 1522]
  Signatures: a–d⁴.

Ludovico degli Arrighi, *Vicentino*, *fl.* 1522.
  La operina di Ludouico Vicentino, da imparare di scriuere littera cancellarescha. [Roma, 1522]
  [32] p. 21 cm.
  Signatures: A–D⁴.
  "Finisce la arte di scriuere littera corsiua ouer cancellarescha. Stampata in Roma per inuentione di Ludouico Vicentino, scritore. Cvm gratia & privilegio.": p. [32]
  The plates were engraved by Ugo da Carpi. A breve of Pope Clemens vii of May 3, 1525, withdrew the privilege from Ludovico and transferred it to Carpi who subsequently published a new enlarged ed. under his own name. Cf. Kristeller in Thieme-Becker, v. 6, p. 48.
  Bound with the author's Il modo de temperare le penne. Roma, 1523.
  1. Penmanship. 2. Alphabets. 3. Lettering. i. Carpi, Ugo da, 1480 (ca.)–1532. ii. Title.
  Z43.A3L83 1522   Rosenwald Coll.   66–89550
  Library of Congress   [2]

AAC 146   NOTES OF WORKS BOUND TOGETHER (cont'd.)

---

979. 1   Ely, Sims, 1909-
E41   The lost Dutchman mine; the story of the
          search for the hidden treasure of the
          Superstition Mountains of Arizona.   New
          York, Macmillan, 1940.
                178 p. illus. 21 cm.   (Lost gold mines
          of the Southwest series)

                Bound with Randall, Edward. Submarine
          treasure. New York, 1953. and Williams, M. E.
          The real book of American tall tales. Garden
          City, N. Y. , 1952.

                1. TREASURE-TROVE--ARIZONA.   I.
          Title (Series)

---

979. 1   Randall, Edward, 1910-
E41   Submarine treasure. Illustrated by
          Hubert Rogers.   New York, Dodd, Mead, 1953.
                vii, 299 p. illus. 21 cm.

                Bound with Ely, Sims. The lost Dutchman
          mine. New York, 1940.
                1st ed. published in 1936 under title:
          Spanish ingots.

                1. Rogers, Hubert, 1891-   illus.
          II. Title. III. Title: Spanish ingots.

---

979. 1   Williams, Mary E   1919-
E41   The real book of American tall tales, by
          Michael Gorham[pseud.] Illustrated by Herbert
          Danska.   Garden City, N. Y. , Garden City
          Books by arrangement with F. Watts, 1952.
                192 p. illus. 21 cm.   (Real books, R30)

                Bound with Ely, Sims. The lost Dutchman
          mine. New York, 1940.

                Includes bibliography.

                1. TALES, AMERICAN. I. Danska,
          Herbert, illus. II. Title.

AAC 147   DISSERTATION NOTE

Anderson, James Richard, 1919–

Some rural land use patterns and problems of Morgan County, Indiana.   ₍College Park, Md.₎ 1950.

210 l.   illus., maps (part fold.)   28 cm.

Thesis—University of Maryland.
Typewritten (carbon copy)
Bibliography : leaves ₍204₎–210.

Williams, Jack Francis.

China in maps, 1890–1960 ; a selective and annotated cartobibliography.   ₍Seattle ?₎ 1966.

viii, 301 l.   maps.   30 cm.

Thesis (M. A.)—University of Washington.
Bibliography : leaves ₍70₎–76.

1. China—Maps—Bibl.   I. Title.

Z6027.C55W5   016.91251   66–93077

Library of Congress   ₍2₎

AAC 149   CONTENTS NOTES

Stendahl, Krister, *ed.*

Immortality and resurrection ; four essays by Oscar Cullmann, Harry A. Wolfson, Werner Jaeger, and Henry J. Cadbury.   New York, Macmillan ₍1965₎

149 p.   18 cm.

Ingersoll lectures given at Harvard University, 1955, 1956, 1958, and 1959.

CONTENTS.—Immortality of the soul or resurrection of the dead? By O. Cullmann.—Immortality and resurrection in the philosophy of the Church Fathers, by H. A. Wolfson.—The Greek ideas of immortality, by W. Jaeger.—Intimations of immortality in the thought of Jesus. by H. J. Cadbury.

1. Immortality — Addresses, essays, lectures.   2. Resurrection—Addresses, essays, lectures.   I. Title.   (Series : The Ingersoll lecture, Harvard University, 1955, etc.)

BT923.S74   291.23   65–17522

Library of Congress   ₍5₎

AAC 149   CONTENTS NOTES (cont'd.)

Terrell, John Upton, 1900–
    War for the Colorado River.   Glendale, Calif., A. H.
Clark Co., 1965.

2 v. maps. 24 cm. (Western lands and waters series, 4–5)

Includes bibliographies.

CONTENTS.—v. 1. The California-Arizona controversy.—v. 2. Above
Lee's Ferry.

Cronin, Vincent.
    The romantic way. [1st American ed.] Boston, Hough-
ton Mifflin, 1966 [°1965]

287 p. illus., ports. 22 cm.

First published in 1965 under title: Four women in pursuit of
an ideal.
Bibliography: p. 277–279.
CONTENTS.—Prologue.—Caroline de Berry.—Marie d'Agoult.—Eve
Hanska.—Marie Bashkirtseff.

1. Berry, Marie Caroline Ferdinande Louise de Naples, duchesse
de, 1798–1870. 2. Agoult, Marie Catherine Sophie (de Flavigny)
comtesse d', 1805–1876. 3. Hańska, Ewelina (hrabina Rzewuska)
afterwards Mme. de Balzac, 1804 or 6–1882. 4. Bashkīrt͡seva, Marīi͡a
Konstantīnovna, 1860–1884.   I. Title.

Mitchell, Allan.
    Revolution in Bavaria, 1918–1919; the Eisner regime and
the Soviet Republic.   Princeton, N. J., Princeton University Press, 1965.

x. 374 p. illus., maps. 21 cm.

Bibliography: p. 347–361.

1. Bavaria—Hist.—1918–1945. 2. Eisner, Kurt, 1867–1919.
I. Title.

DD801.B42M5   943.3   65–10834

Library of Congress   [3]

AAC 149　　CONTENTS NOTES (cont'd.)

Olson, Robert Goodwin, 1924–
　　The morality of self-interest [by] Robert G. Olson.　New
York, Harcourt, Brace & World [1965]

　　x, 182 p.　22 cm.　(An Original harbinger book)

　　Bibliographical footnotes.

Pauly, Reinhard G
　　Music in the classic period [by] Reinhard G. Pauly.
Englewood Cliffs, N. J., Prentice-Hall [1965]

　　214 p.　illus., facsims., map, music.　22 cm.　(Prentice-Hall history
of music series)

　　Bibliographies at end of chapters.

Nettl, Bruno, 1930–
　　Folk and traditional music of the western continents.
Englewood Cliffs, N. J., Prentice-Hall [1965]

　　213 p.　illus., music.　22 cm.　(Prentice-Hall history of music
series)

　　Includes bibliographies and discographies.

　　1. Folk music—America.　ɪ. Title.

　　ML3549.N5　　　　　　　784.4　　　　　　65—17798/MN

　　Library of Congress　　　　[69p5]

AAC 149   CONTENTS NOTES (cont'd.)

Miller, William D
    Mr. Crump of Memphis ₍by₎ William D. Miller.   Baton
Rouge, Louisiana State University Press, 1964.

    xiii, 373 p.   illus., ports.   24 cm.   (Southern biography series)

    "Critical essay on authorities" : p. 353–359.

U. S. *War dept.*
    Infantry drill regulations, United States Army.   1911,
corrected to April 15, 1917 (changes, nos. 1–19)   Washington, Govt. print. off., 1917.

    254 p.   illus., plates, fold. diagr.   15 cm.

    Appendix C : Manual of the bayonet, 1913.
    War dept. doc. no. 394.

Sulzberger, Cyrus Leo, 1912–
    Unfinished revolution : America and the third world ₍by₎
C. L. Sulzberger.   ₍1st ed.₎   New York, Atheneum, 1965.

    304 p.   22 cm.

    Errata slip inserted.

    1. World politics—1965–   2. States, New.   3. Underdeveloped
    areas.   I. Title.

    D843.S86   327   65–15916

    Library of Congress   ₍5₎

AAC 150 "TITLE ROMANIZED" NOTE

Russia (*1923–* U. S. S. R.) *Laws, statutes, etc.*
Директивы КПСС и Советского правительства по хозяй-
ственным вопросам, 1917–1957 годы ; ⌊сборник документов.
Составители : В. Н. Малин и А. В. Коробов⌋ Москва, Гос.
изд-во полит. лит-ры, 1957–58.
    4 v. 23 cm.
    Includes legislation of R. S. F. S. R.
    CONTENTS.—т. **1.** 1917–1928 годы.—т. **2.** 1929–1945 годы.—т. **3.**
1946–1952 годы.—т. **4.** 1953–1957 годы.
    1. Russia — Economic policy — 1917–   2. Industrial laws and
legislation—Russia.   I. Malin, V. N. II. Korobov, A. V. III. Kom-
munisticheskaíà partiíà Sovetskogo Soíùza. IV. Russia (1917–
R. S. F. S. R.) Laws, statutes, etc. v. Title.
          Title transliterated: Direktivy KPSS i Sovetskogo pra-
          vitel'-   stva po khozíaĭstvennym voprosam.

                                            58—19225

Library of Congress   ⌊60r59d1⌋

Kim, Sŏg-yŏng, *ed.*
申翼熙先生一代記　金夕影編　서울　早稻田大
學同窓會　檀紀4289 ⌊1956⌋
    125 p.　port.　18 cm.

    1. Sin, Ik-hi, 1892–1956.
               Title romanized: Sin Ik-hŭi Sŏnsaeng ildaegi.

DS916.5.S5K5   K 58–6 rev ‡

Library of Congress   ⌊r62b⅜⌋

III. Searching

A. Techniques and Tools

The process of searching may be defined as that
process which determines whether or not a particular
book, serial, pamphlet, etc. is a part of the holdings of
a library, a group of libraries or even a special collection.
In order to search a title, the ownership records of the
library are consulted. Although there are many possibilities for the form of such records, they are traditionally
in the form of a catalog. Most catalogs are arranged so
that an author, title or subject may be used as an access
point for the search. In many cases searching also in-
volves determining whether or not a particular title is on
order by the library. This may mean searching both the
library catalog and the order files in the acquisitions department. Because of the problems involved with main
entry, it is often wiser to search by title than by author.
Further searching by subject is difficult as the exact subject heading(s) assigned to a book may not be readily determined. When the search for a particular title is suc-
cessful, the complete call number is usually recorded on
the request or search slip. In addition, the bibliographic
information on the request slip should be completed and
corrected if possible. If there is no record of the
searched title in the library's holding, the next step is
verification of the title.

B. Types of Catalogs

There are basically three types of catalogs according
to physical format: the book catalog, the sheaf catalog,
and the card catalog. The most common of these prior to
the last quarter of the nineteenth century was the book
catalog. It permits any kind of arrangement of entries;
entries may be easily scanned within the volumes; it does
not require an undue amount of space; and there may be as
many copies printed as desired. In fact, in many aspects

the book catalog is the most desirable form of catalog.
Its only serious weakness is in being current.   The addition of new entries requires either supplements or a new
entire printing.   Today this form of catalog is becoming
feasible again within the many possibilities of automation
and its applications to printed book catalogs.   The sheaf
catalog is a loose-leaf catalog which formally was widely
used in Great Britain.   It is similar to the card catalog
except that slips of paper are used in loose-leaf binders
instead of cards in trays.   Its greatest disadvantage is its
size.

     The entries may be arranged in any fashion in any
type of catalog.   The most common type of arrangement
is an alphabetical one.   There are two possibilities in this
case.   All the entries may be arranged in a single alphabet of authors, titles, subjects, etc.   This form is called
the dictionary catalog.   If the subject cards are filed in a
separate tray, you will have a divided catalog.   Divided
catalogs consist of two parts: an author-title catalog and
a subject catalog.   This type of arrangement has many
advantages in relation to filing problems.

     Besides the alphabetical arrangement of entries, it
is possible to have a classified arrangement of subject
entries.   This is called the classed catalog.   The classed
catalog consists of three parts: the classed catalog, the
author-title catalog, and the alphabetical index to the
classification scheme.   The classed catalog is arranged
according to the classification scheme used for the collection of materials.   In short, this gives you a form
(actually an expanded form) of a catalog arranged in the
same fashion as the material is shelved or organized.
Very few libraries in this country maintain a classed catalog.   It is considered too complex for many users to
understand; in addition, it is more expensive to maintain
than a dictionary or divided catalog.

     The most common type of card record maintained
by libraries is the public catalog.   This is the catalog that
is available for the users to consult.   In addition to this
catalog there may be several more catalogs of sorts main-
tained by the cataloging department for internal use.
Practically all libraries have a shelf list in the cataloging
department.   This is a card record arranged according to
the classification scheme of the library.   Each call number is given a separate card, filed in classification order.

In addition, some cataloging departments still maintain
an official catalog which may be an exact duplicate of the
public catalog or may simply be a main entry catalog.
There are also three possible authority files which may
be generated in a cataloging department.   These are a
name or author authority file, a subject authority file,
and a series authority file.   The name authority file
demonstrates the source of the verified form of the author's
name as used for the main entry in the card catalog.
However, many libraries today no longer maintain all
these authority files.

C.   The Unit Card

The unit card system is a system of providing multiple entries for a work by using a basic or unit card and
then duplicating as many additional cards as are necessary.
The unit card is usually a simple main entry card with
complete description and identification of the individual
material.   In addition, the unit card carries a record of
all secondary entries for the individual material.   These
secondary entries may be typed or printed above the main
entry on separate copies of the unit card.   Prior to 1901,
when the Library of Congress began to sell its printed
cards, libraries used hand-written or typed cards.   At
that time only the main entry card was fully descriptive
and the secondary cards were highly abbreviated.   When
the Library of Congress began to sell printed cards in
1901, the unit card system was begun.   Libraries could
buy as many copies of a unit card as necessary and merely
add the secondary entries to them.   Some libraries prefer
to buy only one card and reproduce their own card sets by
some duplicating process.   Today some libraries prefer to
subscribe to proofs of the Library of Congress cards.
These are called proof sheets and are printed on paper
rather than on card stock.

D.   History of Cataloging Rules

The first significant modern rules include Panizzi's
91 Rules for the author catalogue of the British Museum
published in 1841, and Jewett's modifications in the
Smithsonian Report on construction of catalogs in 1852.
It was not until 1876 that Charles Ammi Cutter published
the first complete set of rules for a dictionary catalog.

This work went through four editions before Mr. Cutter's death in 1903. These rules were expanded, revised and changed by the Library of Congress Rules on Printed Cards issued between 1903 and the mid thirties on separate printed cards. In 1908 the first edition of the ALA Rules was issued as another revision of Cutter. This was followed by the Preliminary Second Edition of the ALA Rules, in 1941; the 1949 ALA Rules for Author and Title Entries; the 1949 LC Rules for Descriptive Cataloging; and the new Anglo-American Cataloging Rules in 1967. Similarly, codes developed in other countries, as may be noted in the bibliography of the 1961 Report of International Conference on Cataloging Principles.

E. The Main Entry

1. Possible forms

The main entry may occur in four possible forms. It may be a personal author, a corporate author, a uniform title, or even a title entry. Personal authors are the most common form of main entry. A corporate entry is the entry under some corporate body such as a society, association, or institution which is chiefly responsible for the existence of the work. The third possibility is entry under a uniform title, as for example "Mother Goose". Finally, if none of the above may be chosen for main entry, then a work may be entered under its own title. In this last case the heading and the body are combined and hanging indention is used.

2. Verification Process

There are two ways used by catalogers to determine or establish the correct form of a main entry--whether it is a personal author, a corporate author, or a uniform title. The first method may be called verification. In this case a cataloger must determine the correct form by consulting one or more bibliographical authorities. The two most common authorities are the Library of Congress Printed Catalogs and the Cumulative Book Index. The verifier must take care not to be confused by these two sources. Occasionally there will be variations as to how an individual name is entered. In cases of doubt it is usually better to follow the Library of Congress practice. In addition, there are many other possible biographical

dictionaries and directories which may be used for verification purposes.

3. The Use of Cataloging Codes

The other method of establishing the proper form
for main entries is to use the rules given in the standard
cataloging codes, of which the Anglo-American Rules is
our present one.   By using rules and principles the cataloger will also have to consult bibliographical sources.
According to the new code there are first two decisions
that must be made.   First the author, i. e. the main entry, must be chosen; and, second, the correct form for
this main entry must be established.   There are four
basic principles for the choice of the main entry: first,
enter under author if possible, whether personal or corporate; second, if you cannot enter under author, enter under
the editor; third, if neither author or editor are discerni-
ble, enter under the compiler; and fourth, if none of the
above may be chosen, enter under the title.

The form of the main entry has three different possibilities: personal author, corporate author, and uniform
title.   The new code gives preference to the form of the
personal author's name as used in English language reference sources.   Corporate authors may be entered directly
under their names unless they must be entered under one
of the three following instances.   First, if the name of
the lesser body is non-distinctive, enter under the higher
body.   Second, enter under the governmental name all
corporate bodies which are governmental agencies if they
perform basic legislative, executive, or judicial functions.
Third, enter under place name a corporate body that is a
local church or an educational institution, library, etc. ,
with no distinctive name.   In most cases, entry under uniform title will require careful bibliographical searching.

4. Application of Cataloging Rules

All the processes of cataloging are standardized by
certain rules and conventions so that all patrons will re-
cognize and identify the elements for which they are
searching.   Proper forms of names must be established
by certain criteria.   If this were not done, books by the
same author under different forms of his name would be
difficult to find.   As most patrons of libraries will look
for specific books under author or title, accuracy in

establishing these, as in other aspects of cataloging, is of
utmost importance.   The only other approach the patron
has to the collection is to search for books under subjects.
This third important part of the dictionary catalog is dis-
cussed in the following chapters.   The basic code for both
rules of authorship and descriptive cataloging is the Anglo-
American Cataloging Rules.   This work is a revision of
both the ALA Cataloging Rules for Author and Title Entries and the Rules for Descriptive Cataloging of the Library of Congress.

This chapter is designed to introduce the student to
the authorship rules, descriptive cataloging rules and some
theoretical concepts of cataloging.   After each selection
of rules, there are sections of example cards.

One major problem that all catalogers and library
users will have as a result of the new authorship rules is
pointed out in the following statement from the LC Cataloging Service, Bulletin 79, January 1967.

> The great size of the Library of Congress cata-
> logs and of the catalogs of the research libraries
> that depend on LC cataloging services, the con-
> tinuing shortage of trained cataloging personnel,
> and the emergence of centralized cataloging and
> shared cataloging techniques have made it incum-
> bent on the Library to approach the use of the new
> rules with due consideration of their effect upon
> the catalogs and cataloging activities of all Ameri-
> can libraries.   Accordingly, the Library of Con-
> gress has adopted a policy known as 'Superimpo-
> sition' in applying the new rules.   This means
> that the rules for choice of entry will be applied
> only to works that are new to the Library and
> that the rules for headings will be applied only
> to persons and corporate bodies that are being
> established for the first time.   New editions, etc.,
> of works previously cataloged will be entered in
> the same way as the earlier editions (except for
> revised editions in which change of authorship is
> indicated).   New works by previously established
> authors will appear under the same headings.

The implication of this statement on all the following
rules is most important.   If the rule caused a change in

the established headings, the cataloger should carefully review what this change will mean.

III. Searching: Outline

A. <u>Techniques and tools</u>

B. <u>Kinds of catalogs</u>

    1. Physical format

        a. Book
        b. Sheaf
        c. Card

    2. Arrangement of entries

        a. Alphabetical
           (1) Dictionary
           (2) Divided
              (a) Author-title
              (b) Subject
        b. Classed catalog
           (1) Numerical
           (2) Alphabetical
              (a) Author-title
              (b) Subject index to classed catalog

    3. Types of card records maintained by libraries

        a. Public catalog
        b. Shelf list
        c. Official catalog
        d. Authority files
           (1) Author
           (2) Subject
           (3) Series

    4. Introduction to filing and filing rules

C. <u>History of cataloging rules</u>

    1. Early practices

        a. Established customs
        b. Panizzi's 91 Rules

   2. Rules for dictionary catalogs

        a. Charles Ammi Cutter
        b. 1908 ALA Rules
        c. LC Rules on Printed Cards
        d. 1941 Preliminary 2d ed. of ALA Rules
        e. 1949 ALA Rules for Author and Title Entries
        f. 1949 LC Rules for Descriptive Cataloging
        g. 1961 International Conference on Cataloging
           Principles
        h. 1967 Anglo-American Cataloging Rules

D. Rules of authorship
  (AAC 1, 2, 3, 4, 5, 7, 14, 15, 17, 18, 19, 20, 22, 25, 33)

   1. Choice of entry

        a. Authors
           (1) Individual authorship, personal or corporate
           (2) Shared authorship
         b. Editors
        c. Compilers
        d. Works of non-prescriptive authorship
           (1) Title of the work (handing indention)
           (2) Uniform titles
           (3) Form headings

   2. Form of entry

        a. Personal names
           (AAC 40, 41, 42, 44, 46, 47, 49, 50, 52, 53)
           (1) Common form in English-language reference
              sources
           (2) Special practices for names in non-Roman
              alphabets
        b. Corporate bodies
           (AAC 60, 61, 62, 63, 64, 65, 66, 69, 70, 71,
           72, 73, 74, 75, 77, 78, 79, 80, 81, 83, 87,
           93, 95, 98, 99)
           (1) Distinctive names
           (2) Non-distinctive subordinate names
           (3) Government bodies
              (a) Basic executive, legislative, or judicial
              (b) Others

(4) Special practices for entry by place
c. Uniform titles
(AAC 100, 102, 108, 119)
(1) Anonymous classics
(2) Form titles
(3) Variant editions with conventional titles

III.   Searching: Readings

A.   Techniques and tools,   and B.   Kinds of catalogs

Basic Readings

Lowy,   George,   A Searcher's Manual.   Hamden,   Conn. :
    Shoe String Press,   1965.

Mann,   Margaret.   Introduction to Cataloging and the Clas-
    sification of Books.   2d ed.   Chicago: American Li-
    brary Association,   1943.   Pp.   1-11;   100-117;   171-180;
    181-188.

Wynar,   Bohdan S.   Introduction to Cataloging and Classi-
    fication.   3d ed.   Rochester,   N. Y. :   Libraries Un-
    limited,   1967.
    Pp.   1-6;   274-279.

Enrichment Readings

ALA Rules for Filing Catalog Cards.   Prepared by the
    ALA Editorial Committee's Subcommittee on the
    ALA Rules for Filing Catalog Cards,   Pauline A.
    Seely,   Chairman and Editor.   2d ed.   Abridged.
    Chicago: American Library Association,   1968.

Eaton,   Thelma.   Cataloging and Classification;   an Intro-
    ductory Manual.   4th ed.   Ann Arbor,   Mich. :   Ed-
    wards Brothers,   1967.
    Pp.   1-8.

Grosser,   Dorothy.   "The Divided Catalog: A Summary of
    the Literature, "   Library Resources and Technical
    Services,   2:238-252,   Fall 1958.

Jolley,   Leonard.   The Principles of Cataloguing.   New
    York: Philosophical Library,   1961.
    Pp.   1-11.

Ranz, Jim. The Printed Book Catalogue in American Libraries: 1723-1900. Chicago: American Library Association, 1964. (ACRL Monograph Number 26)

Sayers, W. C. Berwick. An Introduction to Library Classification; Theoretical, Historical and Practical, with Readings, Exercises and Examination Papers, 9th ed. London: Grafton, 1954.
Pp. 192-200.

Shera, Jesse H. and Margaret Egan. The Classified Catalog, Basic Principles and Practices. Chicago: American Library Association, 1956.
Pp. 1-21; 64-103.

Stewart, James Douglas. The Sheaf Catalogue, a Practical Handbook on the Compilation of Manuscript Catalogues for Public and Private Libraries. London: Libraco Limited, 1909.

Tauber, Maurice. Technical Services in Libraries: Acquisitions, Cataloging, Classification, Binding, Photographic Reproduction, and Circulation Operations. New York: Columbia University Press, 1954.
Pp. 109-130.

C. Methods of Entry

Basic Readings

Mann, Margaret. Introduction to Cataloging and the Classification of Books. 2d ed. Chicago: American Library Association, 1943.
Pp. 221-232.

Wynar, Bohdan S. Introduction to Cataloging and Classification. 3d ed. Rochester, N.Y.: Librarian Unlimited, 1967.
Pp. 6-14; 272-274.

Enrichment Readings

Bidlack, Russell E. Typewritten Catalog Cards, A Manual of Procedure and Form with 125 Sample Cards. Ann Arbor, Mich.: Ann Arbor Publishers, c1959.

Columbia University.   School of Library Service.   <u>Sample</u>
    <u>Catalog Cards, for Use in Connection with Courses in</u>
    <u>Technical Services in Libraries and Organization of</u>
    <u>Materials.</u>   3d ed.   New York: 1958.

Colvin, Laura C.   <u>Cataloging Sampler, a Comparative and</u>
    <u>Interpretive Guide.</u>   Hamden, Conn.:   Shoe String
    <u>Press, 1963.</u>

Eaton, Thelma.   <u>Cataloging and Classification; an Intro-</u>
    <u>ductory Manual.</u>   4th ed.   Ann Arbor, Mich.:   Ed-
    <u>wards Brothers, 1967.</u>
    Pp. 9-57.

U. S. Library of Congress.   Descriptive Cataloging Division.
    "Form of Authority Cards, " <u>Cooperative Cataloging</u>
    <u>Manual for the Use of Contributing Libraries.</u>   Wash-
    ington: Govt. Print. Off., 1944.
    Pp. 27-38.

D.   <u>History of Cataloging Rules</u>

Basic Reading

Daily, Jay E.   "Anglo-American Code, " <u>Encyclopedia of</u>
    <u>Library and Information Science.</u>   New York: Marcel
    <u>Dekker, 1968.</u>   Vol. I:416-422.

Supplemental Reading

Osborn, Andrew D.   "The Crisis in Cataloging, "   <u>Library</u>
    <u>Quarterly</u>   11:393-411, 1941.

E.   <u>Rules of authorship</u>

Basic Readings

<u>Anglo-American Cataloging Rules,</u> prepared by the Ameri-
    can Library Association, the Library of Congress,
    the Library Association, and the Canadian Library
    Association.   North American Text.   Chicago:
    American Library Association, 1967.
    Pp. 1-186.   British text, pp. 1-156.

Mann, Margaret, Introduction to Cataloging and the Classification of Books. 2d ed. Chicago: American Library Association, 1943.
Pp. 118-135.

Wynar, Bohdan S. Introduction to Cataloging and Classification. 3d ed. Rochester, N.Y.: Libraries Unlimited, 1967.
Pp. 34-109.

Enrichment Readings

American Library Association. Division of Cataloging and
Classification. A.L.A. Cataloging Rules for Author
and Title Entries. Clara Beetle, ed. 2d ed. Chicago:
American Library Association, 1949.

Cataloging Rules of the American Library Association and
the Library of Congress: Additions and Changes,
1949-58. Washington: The Library of Congress,
1959.
Pp. 1-57.

Field, F. Bernice. "The New Catalog Code: The General
Principles and the Major Changes," Library Resources and Technical Services, 10:421-436, Fall
1966.

Jolley, Leonard. The Principles of Cataloguing. New York:
Philosophical Library, 1961. Pp. 12-97.

Osborn, Andrew D. "AA Cataloging Code," Library Journal,
93:3523-3525, October 1, 1968.

Tauber, Maurice. Technical Services in Libraries: Acquisitions, Cataloging, Classification, Binding, Photographic Reproduction, and Circulation Operations.
New York: Columbia University Press, 1954. Pp.
131-149.

III. Searching: Worksheets

Use of the Card Catalog

1. What is Eric Moon's contribution to Book Selection and Censorship in the Sixties?

2. Under what heading are books about the late John Fitzgerald Kennedy listed?

3. What is the subtitle of Elmer D. Johnson's Communication?

4. The Prussian Instructions was translated from the German by whom?

5. Do you find books entered in the catalog under the name of Harold Lancour?

6. How are novels about the Civil War located in the catalog?

7. Does this library list any books on "Classed Catalogs"?

8. What are the birth and death dates of Charles Ammi Cutter?

9. Are all the books on "Classification" listed under this particular heading?

10. How many biographies of Melvil Dewey are available?

   Who are the authors?

11. How does this library list books written by Lewis Carroll?

12. What is the entry for works of:

   a. Marguerite de Angeli

b.   Vincent Van Gogh

c.   Charles de Gaulle

13.   What is the latest book in the library about Colon
      Classification?

14.   Is Cataloging and Classification, by Bohdan Wynar,
      illustrated?

15.   Does the library have a copy of Julius Kaiser's
      "Systematic Indexing"?

16.   How can you locate a bibliography on acquisitions?

Analysis of Rules of Authorship

Analyze the following 21 LC entries for rules of choice and rules of form. There should be at least one rule of choice taken from the first chapter of AAC for each entry. Second, there should be at least one rule of form taken from the second, third, or fourth chapter of AAC unless the entry is a title (hanging indention) entry. There are no rules of form for title entries. If there is no appropriate AAC rule consult the ALA Cataloging Rules for Author and Title Entries.

Riding, Laura, 1901–
    Lives of wives, by Laura Riding. New York, Random house ₁1939₁

323 p.   22 cm.

Three historical novels, the first dealing with the period of the founding of the Persian empire, the second with the time of Alexander and Aristotle, and the third with the time of Herod the Great. The events of each period are portrayed through the lives of the wives of the principal male characters.   *cf.* Foreword.
"First published 1939."

CONTENTS.—A Persian lady, and her contemporaries. — Macedonian times.—New ways in Jerusalem.

1. History, Ancient—Fiction.   I. Title.

PZ3.R437Li   40—2378

Library of Congress   ₁15₁

Harbeck, Richard Merle, 1923–
    Exploring science in your home laboratory, by Richard Harbeck. Illus. and photos. by the author. New York, Four Winds Press ₁1963₁

128 p.   illus.   20 cm.

1. Laboratories—Juvenile literature.   2. Science—Experiments—Juvenile literature.   I. Title.

Q163.H27   j 507.8   65—29527

Library of Congress   ₁68g3₁

Priestley, Joseph, 1733-1804.
    Writings on philosophy, science, and politics. Edited, with an introd. by John A. Passmore. [1st ed.] New York, Collier Books [1965]

    352 p. 18 cm. (A Collier books original, 06677)

    Collier classics in the history of thought.
    Bibliography: p. 341-343.

    I. Title.

AC7.P69   1965   081   64-22682

Library of Congress   [3]

Fanon, Frantz, 1925-1961.
    The wretched of the earth. Pref. by Jean-Paul Sartre. Translated from the French by Constance Farrington. New York, Grove Press [1965, ^c1963]

    255 p. 21 cm.

    1. France—Colonies—Africa.   2. Algeria—Hist.—1945-
    3. Offenses against the person.   I. Title.

DT33.F313   301.24   65-14196

Library of Congress   [5]

Mayor, John Roberts.
    Accreditation in teacher education: its influence on higher education [by] John R. Mayor [and] Willis G. Swartz. Washington, National Commission on Accrediting [1965]

    xvi, 311 p. 23 cm.

    "A report ... to the National Commission on Accrediting."
    Bibliography: p. 299-303.

    1. Teachers' colleges—Accreditation.   I. Swartz, Willis G., joint author. II. National Commission on Accrediting. III. Title.

LB1811.M26   370.732   65-19290

Library of Congress   [20]

Miller, Alden Holmes, 1906–
    The lives of desert animals in Joshua Tree National Monument [by] Alden H. Miller [and] Robert C. Stebbins. Illustrated by Gene M. Christman. Berkeley, University of California Press, 1964.

    vi, 452 p. illus. (part col.) fold. col. map. 27 cm.

    Bibliography: p. 435–441.

        1. Desert fauna. 2. Zoology—Joshua Tree National Monument.
    I. Stebbins, Robert Cyril, 1915–   joint author. II. Title.

QL116.M5   591.9095   64–18643

Library of Congress   [7–1]

Spigel, Irwin M   *ed.*
    Readings in the study of visually perceived movement [by] Irwin M. Spigel. New York, Harper & Row [1965]

    ix, 347 p. illus. 22 cm.

    Includes bibliographical references.

        1. Motion perception (Vision)   I. Title. II. Title: Visually perceived movement.

BF241.S68   152.1425   65—19491

Library of Congress   [66f5]

Deer, Irving, *ed.*
    Languages of the mass media, readings in analysis. Edited by Irving and Harriet Deer. Boston, D. C. Heath [1965]

    viii, 108 p. 21 cm. (Uses of English; a series for college composition)

    Bibliography: p. 107–108. Bibliographical footnotes.

        1. Mass media—U. S.   I. Deer, Harriet, joint ed. II. Title.

P92.U5D4   301.243   65–14110

Library of Congress   [3]

Tibbetts, D. C.
A bibliography on cold weather construction, compiled by
D. C. Tibbetts. Rev. by G. G. Boileau. Ottawa, Division
of Building Research, National Research Council. 1965.

1 v. (various pagings) 28 cm. (National Research Council,
Canada. Division of Building Research. Bibliography no. 10)
unpriced

(CG 52–64 rev.)

1. Civil engineering—Cold weather conditions—Bibl. i. Boileau,
G. G. ii. Title. (Series)

Z5851.T48

67–86151

McNair, Arnold Duncan McNair, *baron,* 1885–
Legal effects of war. 3d ed. Cambridge [Eng.] University Press, 1948.

xxiii, 458 p. 23 cm.

1. Trading with the enemy. 2. Enemy property. 3. Aliens—Gt.
Brit. 4. Impossibility of performance — Gt. Brit. 5. World War,
1939–1945—Law and legislation—Gt. Brit. i. Title.

48–4163 rev*

La Farge, Christopher, 1897–
... The sudden guest... New York, Coward-McCann, inc.
[1946]

4 p. l., 3–250 p. 21½ cm.

i. Title.

PZ3.L1287Su

46—6673

Bibliographical society of America.
Census of fifteenth century books owned in America ; comp.
by a committee of the Bibliographical society of America.
New York, 1919.

xxiv, 245 p. 27½ cm.

"Reprinted with additions ... from the Bulletin of the New York
public library of April–Dec. 1918 : Aug. 1919."
Introduction signed : George Parker Winship.

1. Incunabula—Bibl.—Catalogs.   ɪ. Winship, George Parker, 1871–
ɪɪ. New York. Public library. ɪɪɪ. Title.

Z240.B59   19—16475

Library of Congress   ₍65j½₎

New York (*State*) *University. Committee on Public Library Service.*
Report of the Commissioner of Education's Committee on
Public Library Service, 1957. Albany, 1958.
196 p. 23 cm.

1. Libraries—New York (State) 2. Library surveys.

Z732.N7N74   027.4747   A 58–9151 ‡

New York.   State Libr.
for Library of Congress   ₍2₎†

Oregon. University. *Library.*
Biological serials. Eugene, 1966.

172 p.   28 cm.   (University of Oregon Library occasional paper
no. 4)

1. Biology—Period.—Bibl.   ɪ. Title.   (Series : Oregon. University. Library. Occasional paper no. 4)

Z881.O675 no. 4   016.574′05   67–63731

Library of Congress   ₍3₎

American Standards Association. *Sectional Committee on Standardization in the Field of Library Work and Documentation, Z39.*
American standard basic criteria for indexes. Sponsor: Council of National Library Associations. Approved May 5, 1959. ₁New York₁ 1959.

11 p. 28 cm.

"ASA Z39.4—1959."
Bibliography: p. 9–11.

1. Indexing. 2. Standardization — Indexes. ı. Council of National Library Associations. ıı. Title: Basic criteria for indexes.

Z695.9.A53   029.5   59–4500 rev

Library of Congress   ₁r61k4₁

Landau, Martin, *ed.*
Management information technology: recent advances and implications for public administration; a symposium based upon papers presented at the 1964 National Conference on Public Administration, New York City, April 17, 1964. ₁Philadelphia₁ Fels Institute of Local and State Government, University of Pennsylvania, 1965.
iii, 53 p. illus. 28 cm.
Conference sponsored by the American Society for Public Administration.
Includes bibliographical references.

1. Electronic data processing — Public administration. 2. U. S.— Executive departments—Management. ı. National Conference on Public Administration,   New York, 1964. ıı. Title.

JK468.A8L3   350   65–21843

Library of Congress   ₁3₁

Koran. English. Selections.
    The short Koran, designed for easy reading; edited by George M. Lamsa. Chicago, Ziff-Davis [1949]
    xx, 377 p. 21 cm.

    I. Lamsa, George Mamishisho, 1893- ed.

Ranganathan festschrift. New York, Asia Pub. House
₁1965–

          v. illus., ports. 25 cm. (Ranganathan series in library sci-
ence, 14

     Includes bibliographies.

     CONTENTS.—v. 1. Library science today; papers contributed on the
71st birthday of Dr. S. R. Ranganathan (12th August 1962), edited by
P. N. Kaula.

     1. Library science—Addresses, essays, lectures. 2. Ranganathan,
Shiyali Ramamrita, rao sahib, 1892–   I. Ranganathan, Shiyali
Ramamrita, rao sahib, 1892–   II. Kaula, Prithvi Nath, ed.   (Se-
ries)

Z665.R33   020.8   65–16073

Library of Congress   ₁4–1₁

A **Basic** book collection for junior high schools. ₁1st₁–
     ed. ₁Chicago₁ American Library Association, 1950–

          v. 23 cm. irregular.

     Vol. for 1956 compiled by a subcommittee of the American Library
Association Editorial Committee.
     Editors: 1950–56, E. R. Berner (with M. Sacra, 1950)—1960–
M. V. Spengler.

     1. Reference books—Bibl. 2. Literature—Bibl. 3. School libraries
(High school)   I. Berner, Elsa R., ed.   II. Sacra, Mabel Snyder,
1894–   ed.   III. Spengler, Margaret V., ed.   IV. American Library
Association.   V. American Library Association.   Editorial Committee.

Z1037.B34   028.52   60—7348

Library of Congress   ₁68t⁵3₁

Blancpain, Marc, 1909–
     Le carrefour de la Désolation, roman.   Paris, Flammarion
₁1951₁

     315 p. 19 cm.

     I. Title.

                                        Full name: Marc Benoni Blancpain.

PQ2603.L3345C28   52–15676 ‡

Library of Congress   ₁1₁

          80932   January 1952

The **Elementary** school library collection, phases 1–2–3. General editor: Mary V. Gaver. 1st ed. Newark, N. J., Bro-Dart Foundation [1965]

xv, 848 p. 32 cm.

—— Supplement. General editor: Mary V. Gaver. Newark, N. J., Bro-Dart Foundation [1966]

v. 849–1048 p. 32 cm.

Z1037.E4 1965 Suppl.

1. Children's literature—Bibl.—Catalogs. I. Gaver, Mary Virginia, 1906– ed. II. Bro-Dart Foundation, Newark, N. J.

Z1037.E4 1965   028.52   65–27597 rev

Library of Congress   [r67f7]

Review of AAC Rules

Give the correct form of main entry for each of the following persons, organizations or works. Indicate any cross references and added entries that are required. In each case cite the number of the AAC rule which determines the form of the entry.

AAC Rule

1. Sean O'Casey.

2. The official legislative messages of President Kennedy.

3. The International Federation for Documentation, also know as Federation Internationale de Documentation.

4. The Oxford English Dictionary edited by James A. H. Murray.

5. The Lamont School of Music of the University of Denver.

6. Journal of the Senate of the Legislature of Pennsylvania.

7. Karl von Roche (A German historian).

8. The Norton Anthology of English Literature, edited by M. H. Abrams, general editor, E. Talbot Donaldson, Hallet

AAC Rule

Smith, Robert M.
Adams, and Samuel
Holt Monk.   The editor
of each section is
clearly identified.

9.   Election laws of the
State of New York

10.   Southern Colorado State
College at Pueblo,
Colorado.

11.   Helen Maria Hunt, née
Fiske, later married
to Jackson.

12.   The second edition of a
play by Moss Hart and
George Kaufman.   The
authors' names were
given in reverse order
on the title page of the
first edition.   It is im-
possible to identify the
portion written by each
author.

13.   The J. C. Penney
Company.

14.   The Reverend John
Smith, dates unknown.

15.   Ketti Fring's dramatization of Thomas Wolfe's
novel, Look Homeward
Angel.

16.   The American Library
Association with offices
in Chicago, Illinois.

17.   Miss Edith Hamilton.

AAC Rule

18. Michael Scammell's
    translation of Vladimir
    Nabokov's novel, The
    Gift.

19. A Literary History of
    England, by Kemp
    Malone, Albert C. Baugh,
    Tucker Brooke, George
    Sherburn, and Samuel
    C. Chew, edited, with
    an introduction by Albert
    C. Baugh.   Baugh's
    name appears on the
    title page.

20. The American Theologi-
    cal Library Association
    which is affiliated with
    the American Library
    Association.

21. Mrs. Gregory Bateson
    who has written only
    under the name of
    Margaret Mead.

22. The Library of the
    School of Library Ser-
    vice of Columbia Uni-
    versity.

23. Harley Granville-Barker.

24. The Authoritarian Per-
    sonality, by T. Adorno,
    Eise Frenkel-Brunswick,
    Daniel J. Levison and
    R. Nesbitt Sanford in
    collaboration with Betty
    Aron and William Mor-
    row.

25. The Iowa Chapter of the
    Sons of the American

Revolution.

26. Mrs. H. H. A. Breach; born Amy Marcy Cheney; always used the name of Mrs. H. H. A. Beach on published works.

27. The Bureau of the Mint of the U. S. Treasury Department.

28. The Reverend John B. Phillips.

29. Federico Garcia Lorca.

30. Walter de la Mare (American Author)

31. Wadsworth Public Library of Geneseo, N. Y.

32. Library of the U. S. Department of Agriculture

33. Ernest Gower's revised edition of H. W. Fowler's A Dictionary of Modern Usage.

34. The One-Act Theatre, a Collection of New Comedies and Dramas.

35. The collected letters of Samuel Taylor Coleridge, edited by Henry Nelson Coleridge.

III.   Searching

Samples of Catalog Cards

AAC 1   WORKS OF SINGLE AUTHORSHIP

Powell, Lawrence Clark, 1906–
     The little package; pages on literature and landscape from
a traveling bookman's life.   ₁1st ed.₎   Cleveland. Worl⸱
Pub. Co. ₁1964₎

     316 p.   22 cm.

     Bibliographical footnotes.

     1. Books and reading—Addresses, essays, lectures.   2. Voyages   ₁
travels—Addresses, essays, lectures.   I. Title.

Z1003.P84×5   814.52   64   ₁2⸳⸳₎

Library of Congress   ₁64f2₎

AAC 2   WORKS OF UNKNOWN OR UNCERTAIN
            AUTHORSHIP

A reflection on poetry, by the author
     of The new prose.   London,
     Campbell ₎cl894₎
     46 p. illus. 20 cm.

     I. The new prose, Author of.

Land of the Nile; letters from Cairo,
     by an English lady.   Edited by Mary
     Streete.   New York, Simon and
     Schuster, 1947.
     331 p. illus. 22 cm.

     1.   EGYPT--DESCRIPTION AND TRAVEL.
I. An English lady.   II. Streete, Mary,
1916-   ed.   III. Title:Letters from
Cairo.

AAC 3   WORKS OF SHARED AUTHORSHIP

Tinbergen, Nikolaas, 1907–
    Animal behavior, by Niko Tinbergen and the editors of
Life. New York, Time Inc. ₍1965₎

    200 p.   illus. (part col.) ports. 28 cm.   (Life nature library)

Tonne, Herbert Arthur, 1902–
    Methods of teaching business subjects ₍by₎ Herbert A.
Tonne, Estelle L. Popham ₍and₎ M. Herbert Freeman. 3d
ed. New York, Gregg Division, McGraw Hill Book Co.
₍1965₎

    vi, 488 p. illus. 24 cm.

    Includes bibliographies.

        1. Business education.   I. Popham, Estelle L., joint author.
    II. Freeman, Max Herbert, 1907–   joint author.   III. Title.

Smith, Roger Cletus, 1888–
    Guide to the literature of the zoological sciences, by Roger
C. Smith and Reginald H. Painter. 7th ed. Minneapolis,
Burgess Pub. Co. ₍1967₎

    xiv, 238 p. 26 cm.

        1. Zoology—Bibl.   I. Painter, Reginald Henry, 1901–   joint
    author.   II. Title.   III. Title: Zoological sciences.

    The **Space** encyclopaedia; a guide to astronomy and space
    research. ₍Contributors: Harold Spencer Jones, and others.
    General editor: M. T. Bizony₎ New York, Dutton, 1958
    ₍ᶜ1957₎

        287, 7 p. illus., maps, charts, diagrs. 25 cm.

        1. Astronautics—Dictionaries. 2. Astronomy—Dictionaries.
    I. Bizony, M. T., ed.

    TL788.S6   1958b   629.1388   59—5818

    Library of Congress   ₍61r59f²15₎

WORKS OF SHARED AUTHORSHIP
C.   Joint pseudonyms

Queen, Ellery.
    And on the eighth day.
New York, Random House [1964]
    191 p.   22 cm.

    Ellery Queen is the joint
pseudonym of Frederic Dannay and
Manfred Bennington Lee.

Dannay, Frederic.

    For works of this author written
in collaboration with Manfred Lee
see entries under:

Queen, Ellery

WORKS PRODUCED UNDER EDITORIAL
DIRECTION

Benét, William Rose, 1886–1950, *ed.*
    The reader's encyclopedia. 2d ed. New York, Crowell
    [1965]

Van Nostrand's scientific encyclopedia; aeronautics, astron-
    omy, botany, chemical engineering, chemistry, civil engineer-
    ing, electrical engineering, electronics, geology, guided mis-
    siles, mathematics, mechanical engineering, medicine, metal-
    lurgy, meteorology, mineralogy, navigation, nuclear science
    & engineering, photography, physics, radio & television, sta-
    tistics, zoology. 3d ed. Princeton, N. J., Van Nostrand
    [1958]
        vi, 1839 p.   illus. (part col.) maps, diagrs., tables. 29 cm.

    1. Science—Dictionaries.

    Q121.V3   1958   503   58—7085

    Library of Congress   [68b⁵10]

AAC 5   COLLECTIONS

Wallace, Robert, 1932–   *ed.*
　　Poems on poetry; the mirror's garland, compiled and
edited by Robert Wallace and James G. Taaffe. ₁1st ed.₁
New York, Dutton, 1965.

　　xxii, 328 p. 19 cm.

　　"D159."

　　　1. English poetry (Selections: Extracts, etc.) 2. American poetry
(Selections: Extracts, etc.)   ɪ. Taaffe, James G., joint ed. ɪɪ. Title.

Mississippi black paper; fifty-seven Negro and white citi-
zens' testimony of police brutality, the breakdown of law
and order and the corruption of justice in Mississippi.
Foreword by Reinhold Niebuhr. Introd. by Hodding Carter ɪɪɪ. New York, Random House ₁1965₁

　　92 p. illus. 28 cm.

　　　1. Police — Mississippi. 2. Law enforcement — Mississippi. 3.
Negroes—Mississippi.   ɪ. Title: Fifty-seven Negro and white citi-
zens' testimony of police brutality. ɪɪ. Niebuhr, Reinhold, 1892–

　　HV8145.M7M5   323.11960762   65–18103

　　Library of Congress   ₁8₁

Ellsworth, Ralph Eugene, 1907–
　　Buildings, by Ralph E. Ellsworth. Shelving, by Louis
Kaplan.   Storage warehouses, by Jerrold Orne.   New
Brunswick, N. J., Graduate School of Library Service, Rut-
gers, the State University, 1960.

　　3 v. in 1. 23 cm. (The State of the library art, v. 3)

　　Includes bibliographies.

　　　1. Library architecture.   ɪ. Kaplan, Louis, 1909–   Shelving.
ɪɪ. Orne, Jerrold, 1911–   Storage warehouses.   (Series)

　　Z679.E4   022.082   60—7279

　　Library of Congress   ₁68u3₁

Paperbacks in print.

London, J. Whitaker.

v.   22–25 cm.

Began publication in May 1960 with title Paperbacks.

1. Bibliography—Paperback editions.   I. Whitaker, firm, publishers, London.   II. Title: Paperbacks.

International Congress of Linguists.
Proceedings. 1st–
1928–
[v. p.]

v.   23–27 cm.

Title varies: Actes or Atti.
Contributions in French, English, German, or Italian.

1. Language and languages—Congresses.   2. Linguists.

P21.I 58   30—33923*

Library of Congress   [62r59g½]

Austen, Jane, 1775–1817.
Pride and prejudice; adapted by Ollie Depew, edited by Herbert Spencer Robinson. New York, Globe Book Co. [1951]

325 p. illus. 21 cm.

I. Depew, Ollie, 1888–   II. Title.

PZ3.A93Pr 58   823.74   51–2270

Library of Congress   [2]

Howard, Sidney Coe, 1891-1939.
     Sinclair Lewis' Dodsworth, dram-
atized by Sidney Howard, with comments
by Sidney Howard and Sinclair Lewis on
the art of dramatization...   New York,
Harcourt, 1934.
     lxxii, 162p. illus. 21 cm.

     I. Lewis, Sinclair.   Dodsworth.
II. Title: Dodsworth.

Cunningham, Eileen (Roach) 1894-1965.
     Classification for medical literature. Rev. and enl. by
Eleanor G. Steinke and Mary Louise Gladish. 5th ed.
Nashville, Vanderbilt University Press, 1967.

     xix, 267 p. 25 cm.

     1. Classification—Books—Medicine.   I. Steinke, Eleanor G., ed.
II. Gladish, Mary Louise, ed. III. Title.

Winchell, Constance Mabel, 1896–
     Guide to reference books. 7th ed.   Chicago, American
Library Association, 1951.
     xvii, 645 p. 28 cm.
     "Based on the Guide to reference books, sixth edition, by Isadore
Gilbert Mudge."
———————— Supplement. [1st]–   1950–1952–
Chicago, American Library Association.
     v. 28 cm.
     Vols. for 1950–52 issued in cooperation with O. A. Johnson; 1956–
58—   with J. N. Waddell and others.
               Z1035W79 1951 Suppl.
     1. Reference books—Bibl.   I. Mudge, Isadore Gilbert, 1875–1957.
Guide to reference books. II. American Library Association.

Z1035.W79 1951   016   51—11157

Library of Congress   [68r64u⁶2]

Pirandello, Luigi, 1867–1936.
　　Short stories.　Selected, translated, and introduced by
　Frederick May.　London, New York, Oxford University
　Press, 1965.

　　xxxvi, 260 p.　19 cm.　(Oxford library of Italian classics)
　　Bibliography : p. 231–260.

　　　ɪ. May, Frederick, tr.

Simpson, Jacqueline, *tr.*
　　The Northmen talk; a choice of tales from Iceland.
　Translated and with an introd. by Jacqueline Simpson.
　Foreword by Eric Linklater.　London, Phoenix House;
　Madison, University of Wisconsin Press, 1965.

　　xxix, 290 p.　20 cm.

　　1. Icelandic and Old Norse literature—Translations into English.
　2. English literature—Translations from Icelandic and Old Norse.　3.
　Sagas.　ɪ. Title.

　　PT7221.E5S5　　　　　839.68008　　　　65—16366

　　Library of Congress　　　　₍66d3₎

U. S. *Library of Congress. Subject Cataloging Division.*
　　Subject headings used in the dictionary catalogs of the
　Library of Congress ₍from 1897 through June 1964₎　7th
　ed., edited by Marguerite V. Quattlebaum.　Washington
　₍For sale by the Card Division, Library of Congress₎ 1966.

　　viii, 1432 p.　31 cm.

　　"Additions to and changes in these headings will be found in
　the supplement for July 1964–December 1965, and in monthly and
　cumulative supplements beginning with January 1966."

　　1. Subject headings.　　ɪ. Quattlebaum, Marguerite Rebecca (Voge-
　ding) 1909–

　　Z695.U4749　　　　　　　　　　　　　　65–60043
　　——— ——— Copy 3.　　　Z663.78.S82
　　Library of Congress　　　₍3₎

U. S. President, 1953-1960 (Eisenhower).
   The U. S. in the U. N. [Washing-
ton] Dept. of State [1960]
      8p. illus. 24 cm.   (U. S. Dept. of
State. Publication 7080. International organization and conference series, 16)

"From President Eisenhower's letter
...in the United Nations during 1959."

AAC 18   CORPORATE BODY OR SUBORDINATE UNIT

U. S. *Library of Congress. Aerospace Technology Division.*
   CBE factors; annotated bibliography. no. 1-3. [Wash-
ington] 1965.

   3 no. 28 cm. (*Its* ATD report)

   Covers available Soviet open-source literature on or related to
chemical factors, biological factors, and environmental factors.
   No. 1 is compiled from sources published prior to Dec. 31, 1962;
no. 2-3 from sources published 1963-64.
   Superseded by the Division's CBE factors; monthly survey.

   1. Agricultural chemistry—Bibl. 2. Medicine—Bibl.
   I. Title. (Series)

   Z663.23.A2   65–62280
   ——— ———— 2d set.   TL507.U67

   Library of Congress   [3]

AAC 19   RELATED WORKS

Science abstracts of China. (*Indexes*)
   KWIC index to the Science abstracts of China. 1st ed.
Cambridge, Massachusetts Institute of Technology Libraries,
1960.

   154 p. 28 cm.

   "Prepared for the symposium on the sciences of Communist China
held by the American Association for the Advancement of Science,
December 26-27, 1960, with the aid of a grant from the National
Science Foundation."
   Introd. signed: R. M. Ross, director, Chinese science project,
M. I. T. Libraries.

   1. Science—Abstracts—Indexes.   I. Massachusetts Institute of
Technology. Libraries. II. American Association for the Advancement of Science. III. Title.

   Z7407.C5S3   66–95943

   Library of Congress   [2]

Rosenbaum, Stanford Patrick.
A concordance to the poems of Emily Dickinson, edited
by S. P. Rosenbaum.   Ithaca, N. Y., Cornell University
Press ₁1964₁

xxii, 899 p.   25 cm.   (The Cornell concordances)

1. Dickinson, Emily, 1830–1886—Concordances.   ɪ. Title.
(Series)

PS1541.Z49R6   811.4   64–25335

Library of Congress   ₁5₁

Virginia. *Laws, statutes, etc.*
Code of Virginia, 1950. With provision for subsequent
pocket parts. Annotated. Prepared by the Virginia Code
Commission under authority of chapter 262 of the Acts of
the general assembly of 1948. Charlottesville, Va., Michie
Co. ₁1949–

Denver. Ordinances, local laws, etc.
Zoning ordinances of the city and
county of Denver. Rev. to April 30,
1959.   Denver, Department of Zoning
Administration ₁1959₁
1 v. (loose-leaf) 26 cm.

Denver. Ordinances, etc.
Zoning ordinances of the city and
county of Denver. Rev. to April 30,
1959.   Denver, Department of Zoning
Administration ₁1959₁
1 v. (loose-leaf)   26 cm.

Old
Rule →

1. ZONING LAW--DENVER. I. Denver.
Dept. of Zoning Administration.

Brazil. *Constitution.*
　Constituição federal brazileira; commentarios, por João
Barbalho U. C. Rio de Janeiro, 1902.
　411 p. 28 cm.
　"Constituição de 24 de Fevereiro de 1891."

　　1. Brazil—Constitutional law.　　I. Barbalho Uchôa Cavalcanti,
João, ed. II. Title.

　　　　　　　　　　　　　　　　　　　　　　　　51–52882

　　　Library of Congress　　　⌊1⌋

AAC 25   TREATIES, INTERGOVERNMENTAL
　　　　　　AGREEMENTS, ETC.

U.S. Treaties, etc. Ecuador, Dec. 9, 1958.
　Surplus agricultural commodities.
Agreement between the United States of
America and Ecuador, amending Agreement of
June 30, 1958, effected by exchange of
notes dated at Quito December 9 and 12,
1958.　[Washinton, U.S. Govt. Print.
Off., 1959]
　　3 p. 24 cm.　　(Treaties and other
international acts series, 4166)

U. S. *Treaties, etc., 1953–* 　　(*Eisenhower*)
　Surplus agricultural commodities. Agreement between
the United States of America and Ecuador, amending Agreement of June 30, 1958, effected by exchange of notes dated
at Quito December 9 and 12, 1958. ⌈Washington, U. S. Govt.
Print. Off., 1959⌋
　　3 p. 24 cm. (Treaties and other international acts series, 4166)
　　English and Spanish.

　　1. Surplus agricultural commodities, American — Ecuador.　　I.
Ecuador. Treaties, etc., 1956–　　(Ponce)　　(Series: U. S. Dept.
of State. Treaties and other international acts series, 4166)

　　JX235.9.A32　no. 4166　　　　　　　　59–60536

　　　Library of Congress　　　⌊3⌋

Old
Rule →

Shaw, George Bernard, 1856–1950.
  Collected letters.   Edited by Dan H. Laurence.   New
York, Dodd, Mead ₁1965–

  v. illus., facsims., ports. 25 cm.

  CONTENTS.—₁1₁ 1874–1897.

  I. Laurence, Dan H., ed.

  PR5366.A4 1965   826.912   65–22550

  Library of Congress   ₁5₁

Ruthin, Margaret.
  Katrina of the lonely isles. ₁1st American ed.₁ New York,
Ariel Books ₁1965, ℗1964₁

  162 p. 22 cm.

Bryher, Winifred, 1894–
  Ruan. ₁New York₁ Pantheon Books ₁1960₁

  190 p. illus. 21 cm.

*Old
Rule* →

```
Dodgson, Charles Lutwidge, 1332-1893.
    Alice's adventures in wonderland &
Through the looking glass, both with
the illus. of John Tenniel; & The hunting
of the snark.  All by Lewis Carroll.
New York, F. Watts ₁1964₁
    292 p.  illus.  24 cm.



    I. Title.  II. Title:Through the
looking glass.  III. Title:The hunting
of the snark.
```

Joannes de Garlandia, ca. 1195-ca. 1272.
    Compendivm alchimiae ɾsiue in
Tabulam smaragdinam Hermetic Trismegisti
commentarijɔ...   Basileae, 1560.
    Microfilm copy. Negative.

Horace.
    Odes and epodes, a modern English
verse translation by Joseph P. Clancy.
ɾChicagoɔ University of Chicago Press
ɾ1960ɔ
    v, 257 p.   21 cm.

Euripides.
    Alcestis, translated by Richmond Lattimore. The Medea,
translated by Rex Warner. The Heracleidae, translated by
Ralph Gladstone. Hippolytus, translated by David Grene.
With an introd. by Richmond Lattimore. ɾChicagoɼ University of Chicago Press ɾ1955ɼ

    ix, 220 p. 22 cm. (The Complete Greek tragedies ɾv. 3ɼ)

    Cover title: Four tragedies.

    I. Title. II. Title: The Medea. III. Title: The Heracleidae.
IV. Title: Hippolytus.

PA3975.A2 1955   882.3   55—5787

Library of Congress   ɾ55k10ɼ

Erasmus, Desiderius, *d.* 1536.
    The colloquies of Erasmus. Translated by Craig R.
Thompson. Chicago, University of Chicago Press ɾ1965–

    v. 25 cm.

    Bibliographical footnotes.

    I. Thompson, Craig Ringwalt, 1911-   tr. II. Title.

PA8508.E5T52   879   64-22246

Library of Congress   ɾ3ɼ

COMPOUND SURNAMES

Day-Lewis, Cecil, 1904–
The lyric impulse [by] C. Day Lewis. Cambridge, Harvard University Press, 1965.

164 p. 22 cm. (The Charles Eliot Norton lectures, 1964–1965)

Bibliographical references in "Notes": p. [157]–160.

Cotton, Dorothy (Whyte)
The case for the working mother. New York, Stein and Day [1965]

185 p. 22 cm.

Old Rule →

1. Mothers—Employment.   I. Title.

HD6055.C58   301.4233   65–14395

Library of Congress   [5]

SURNAMES WITH SEPARATELY WRITTEN PREFIXES

De Grazia, Alfred.
Republic in crisis; Congress against the Executive force. [New York] Federal Legal Publications [1965]

303 p. 23 cm.

"Note on methods and sources of Republic in crisis": p. 275–295.

Van Duzer, Henry Sayre, 1853–1928, *comp.*
A Thackeray library; first editions and first publications, portraits, water colors, etchings, drawings and manuscripts. With a new introd. by Lionel Stevenson. Port Washington, N. Y., Kennikat Press, 1965.

198 p. illus., facsims., ports. 24 cm.

"A few additional items are included, forming a complete Thackeray bibliography."

1. Thackeray, William Makepeace, 1811–1863—Bibl.   I. Title.

Z8869.V272   016.8238   65–18612

Library of Congress   [18-1]

SURNAMES WITH SEPARATELY WRITTEN
PREFIXES (cont'd.)

DeFrancis, John Francis, 1911–
 Character text for Intermediate Chinese, by John De-
Francis. New Haven, Published for Seton Hall University
by Yale University Press, 1965.

Croisset, Francis de, 1877–1937.

La Tour-Landry, Geoffroy de, *14th cent.*
 The book of the knight of La Tour-Landry, compiled for

Grimmelshausen, Hans Jacob Christoffel von, 1625–1676.
 The runagate Courage. Translated by Robert L. Hiller

Van Loon, Hendrik Willem, 1882–1944.
 Observations on the mystery of print and the work of
Johann Gutenberg, by Hendrik Willem Van Loon. [New
York] Second national book fair, New York times, Book
manufacturers' institute, 1937.

 6 p. l., 7–45, [2] p. incl. front., illus. 20½ cm.

 Illustrated t.-p.

 1. Printing—Hist.—Origin and antecedents. 2. Gutenberg, Johann,

MacAvoy, Paul W
 The economic effects of regulation; the trunk-line rail-
road cartels and the Interstate Commerce Commission before 1900 [by] Paul W. MacAvoy. Cambridge, Mass.,
M. I. T. Press [1965]

 ix, 275 p. 25 cm.

 Bibliography : p. 267–272.

 1. Railroads—U. S.—Rates. 2. Railroads and state—U. S.
 I. Title.

 HE1843.M19   338.8   65—23542

 Library of Congress   [6715]

TITLES OF NOBILITY, HONOR, ADDRESS, ETC., ADDED TO THE NAME

Bacon, Francis, *viscount St. Albans,* 1561–1626.
Essays, civil, and moral, and The new Atlantis, by Francis Bacon. Aropagitica, and Tractate on education, by John Milton. Religio medici, by Thomas Browne. With

Huxley, *Sir* **Julian Sorell,** 1887–
Charles Darwin and his world, by Julian Huxley and H. B. D. Kettlewell. New York, Viking Press ₁1965₎

144 p. illus., facsims., ports. 24 cm. (A Studio book)

Bonham-Carter, *Lady* **Violet (Asquith)** 1887–
Winston Churchill: an intimate portrait ₍by₎ Violet Bonham Carter. ₍1st American ed.₎ New York, Harcourt, Brace & World ₍1965₎

x, 413 p. illus., ports. 24 cm.

Published, in Great Britain under title: Winston Churchill as I knew him.
Bibliography: p. 387–388.

Anson, *Sir* **William Reynell,** *bart.,* 1843–1914.
Principles of the English law of contract and of agency in its relation to contract. 15th ed. by Maurice L. Gwyer. Oxford, Clarendon Press, 1920.

xxxvii, 458 p. 23 cm.

Stenton, Doris Mary (Parsons) *Lady.*
English justice between the Norman Conquest and the Great Charter, 1066–1215 ₍by₎ Doris M. Stenton. Philadelphia, American Philosophical Society, 1964.

ix, 238 p. illus. 24 cm. (Jayne lectures, 1963)

Memoirs of the American Philosophical Society, v. 60.
Bibliography: p. 216–219.

1. Justice, Administration of—Gt. Brit.—Hist. 2. Law—Gt. Brit.—Sources. I. Title. (Series. Series: American Philosophical Society, Philadelphia. Memoirs, v. 60)

————— Copy 2.

347.9942
Q11.P612 vol. 60

64—14094

Library of Congress ₍66k4₎

Charnwood, John Roby Benson, *baron,* 1901–1955.
　　An essay on binocular vision, by Lord Charnwood.　New
York, Hafner Pub. Co., 1965.

　　117 p.　illus.　24 cm.

　　Bibliography : p. 111–115.

Oxenstierna, Eric Carl Gabriel, *greve,* 1916–
　　The Norsemen ₁by₁ Eric Oxenstierna.　Translated and
edited by Catherine Hutter.　Greenwich, Conn., New York
Graphic Society Publishers ₁1965₁

　　320 p.　illus., maps.　26 cm.

　　Translation of Så levde vikingarna:
　　Bibliography : p. ₁299₁–301.

　　1. Northmen.　　ɪ. Hutter, Catherine, ed. and tr.

　　DL65.O933　　　　　　　909.0974395　　　　　65—16464

　　Library of Congress　　　　　₁67t3₁

```
Elizabeth II, Queen of Great Britain,
        1926-
     Dedication; a selection from the
public speeches of Her Majesty, Queen
Elizabeth II, compiled by Joan Werner
Laurie.     London, Heinemann ₍1953₎
```

```
Alexandra, consort of Peter II, King of
        Yugoslavia, 1921-
     For love of a king.  ₍1st ed.₎
Garden City, N.Y., Doubleday, 1956.
        318 p.  illus.  22 cm.




     1. PETER II, KING OF YUGOSLAVIA,
1923-     I. Title.
```

C. Saints

Benedict, Saint, Abbot of Monte Cassino.
   The rule of Saint Benedict,
translated with an introd. by Cardinal
Gasquet.   London, Chatto & Windus,
1925.
   xxviii, 130 p.   port.   17 cm.
(The Medieval library)

More, Sir Thomas, Saint, 1478-1535.
   Utopia.   Edited with introd. and notes
by Edward Surtz.   New Haven, Yale
University Press, 1964.
   xxxiv, 158 p.   front.   21 cm.   (The
Yale edition of the works of St. Thomas
More: selected works)

   Bibliography: p. xxxi-xxxiv.

   1. UTOPIAS.   I. Surtz, Edward L., ed.

D. Popes

Pius XII, Pope, 1876-1958.
   Guide for living; an approved
selection of letters and addresses of
His Holiness Pope Pius XII, arranged
by Maurice Quinlan.   New York,
Longmans, Green, 1960.
   270 p.   illus.   23 cm.

   1. CATHOLIC CHURCH--ADDRESSES,
ESSAYS, LECTURES.   I. Title.

AAC 52 & 53   GENERAL ADDITIONS TO NAMES

Dinkins, James, *b.* 1845.

Warrack, Alexander, *d.* 1916.

Bradstreet, Anne (Dudley) 1612?–1672.

Brown, James Wilson, Sept. 18, 1913–

Wilhelm, Paul L   1913–
        Criminal law manual for Indiana police, by Paul L. Wilhelm, Sr., Clifford D. Arnold [and] Paul L. Wilhelm, Jr. Michigan City, Ind., Morale Institute, 1965.

        1 v. (loose-leaf)   30 cm.
        Bibliography: p. 207.

Jefferson, George, *writer on librarianship.*
        Public library administration; an examination guidebook.
        [New York] Philosophical Library [1966]
        75 p.   23 cm.

Woodward, Joan, M. A.
        Industrial organization: theory and practice.   London, New York, Oxford University Press, 1965.

        xii, 281 p. illus. 23 cm.
        Bibliographical footnotes.

        1. Industrial management.   I. Title.

        HD31.W64   658.402   65–6145

        Library of Congress   [1]

New York times.
The road to the White House; the story of the 1964 election, by the staff of the New York times. Edited by Harold Faber. ₁1st ed.₎ New York, McGraw-Hill ₁1965₎

xvi, 305 p. illus., ports. 24 cm.

1. Presidents—U. S.—Election—1964.   I. Faber, Harold, ed.
II. Title.

E850.N42   973.923   65—20111

Library of Congress   ₁65f7₎

American Philosophical Society, Philadelphia.
Studies of historical documents in the Library of the American Philosophical Society. Philadelphia, 1959.
727–821 p. illus., facsims. 27 cm.
(*Its* Proceedings, v. 103, no. 6)

Includes bibliographical references.

I. American Philosophical Society, Philadelphia. Library. (Series)

Catholic Church.
The Church teaches; documents of the church in English translation. The selections in this book were translated and prepared for publication by John F. Clarkson [and others of] St. Mary's College, St. Marys, Kansas.
St. Louis, B. Herder [c1955]
xiv, 400 p. 21 cm.

1. CATHOLIC CHURCH--DOCTRINAL AND CONTROVERSIAL WORKS. I. Catholic Church. Canons, decretals, etc. II. Title.

AAC 65   ADDITIONS TO NAMES

National Book League, *London.*
Science for all; an annotated reading list for the non-specialist. Prepared in consultation with British Association for the Advancement of Science. London, 1964.

vii, 251 p. (p. 241–251 advertisements) 19 cm.

1. Science—Bibl.   I. British Association for the Advancement of Science.   II. Title.

Z7401.N324   65–5939

Library of Congress   [2]

AAC 66   OMISSIONS FROM NAMES

Association of American Law Schools.
The law of U. S.-U. S. S. R. trade; papers prepared for Conference of American and Soviet Legal Scholars, June 1965. [Washington, 1965]

103 p.   23 cm.

Cover title.
Bibliographical footnotes.

The News, New York.
European round trip.   [New York,
News Syndicate Co., 1960]
43 p.   illus.   18 cm.

1. SHOPPING--EUROPE.   I. Title.

European Economic Community. *Commission.*
The instruments of monetary policy in the countries of
the European Economic Community. ₁n. p., **Pub. Services**
of the European Communities, 1962₁

268 p.   illus.   25 cm.

Cover title.
At head of title : European Economic Community.

Association of College and Research Libraries. *Buildings*
Committee.
Proceedings of the meetings ₁of the₁ library building
plans institute.   1st–   1952–

Rutgers University, *New Brunswick, N. J.   Graduate School*
of Library Service.
Rutgers series on systems for the intellectual organization
of information.   v. 1–
New Brunswick, 1964–

v.   22 cm.

1. Title.

Z696.A1R8   65–63186

Library of Congress   ₁1₁

Joint Committee on Continuing Legal Education of the
American Law Institute and the American Bar Asso-
ciation.
Consolidated index to five **ALI–ABA** practice handbooks
on the Uniform commercial code.   Philadelphia, ₁1965₁

38 p.   22 cm.

1. Commercial law—U. S.—Indexes.   ɪ. Title.   ɪɪ. Title : Uniform commercial code.

65—22853

Library of Congress   ₁68c1₁

Hamilton, N. Y.
    Community facilities, public utilities and
capital improvements, by Russell D. Bailey,
planning consultant.   Utica, N. Y.,
1959.
        1 v. maps, tables. 29 cm.

New York (State) Dept. of Mental Hygiene.
    Symposium on research into the causes of
feeblemindedness.   Utica, State Hospitals
Press, 1952.

New York (City) Dept. of Parks.
    Six years of park progress. New York,
1940.
        56 p. illus., maps. 23 cm.

    1. NEW YORK (CITY)--PARKS. I. Title.

Russia (*1923–   U. S. S. R.*) *Laws, statutes, etc.*
    Директивы КПСС и Советского правительства по хозяй-
ственным вопросам, 1917–1957 годы ; ¡сборник документов.
Составители: В. Н. Малин и А. В. Коробов¡ Москва, Гос.
изд-во полит. лит-ры, 1957–58.
        4 v. 23 cm.
        Includes legislation of R. S. F. S. R.
        Contents.—т. 1. 1917–1928 годы.—т. 2. 1929–1945 годы.—т. 3.
1946–1952 годы.—т. 4. 1953–1957 годы.
        1. Russia — Economic policy — 1917–   2. Industrial laws and
legislation—Russia.   I. Malin, V. N. II. Korobov, A. V. III. Kom-
munisticheskaíà partiíà Sovetskogo Soíùza. IV. Russia (1917–
R. S. F. S. R.)   Laws, statutes, etc.   v. Title.
                Title transliterated: Direktivy KPSS i Sovetskogo pra-
                    vitel'-   stva po khozíàĭstvennym voprosam.

                                        58—19225

AAC 79   SUBORDINATE AGENCIES AND UNITS

U. S. *Bureau of the Census.*
  Statistical abstract of the United States.   1st–   ed.;
1878–
Washington, U. S. Govt. Print. Off.
    v.   24 cm.   annual.
  The 7th–8th editions combined in one issue; 66th ed., covers period
1944–45.
  Issued 1878–1902 by the Bureau of Statistics (Treasury Dept.) ;
1903–11 by the Bureau of Statistics (Dept. of Commerce and Labor) ;
1912–37 by the Bureau of Foreign and Domestic Commerce.
———— Cities supplement: selected data for cities having
25,000 or more inhabitants.   1940.   Washington.
    ii, 47 p.   27 cm.
  Superseded by its County and city data book, 1949.
                                        HA202   Cities suppl.
    1. U. S.—Stat.   i. Title.
  HA202   -317.3   4—18089*
  Library of Congress   [68r52w²¹5]

AAC 80   GOVERNMENT OFFICIALS

U. S. President, 1953-1960 (Eisenhower)
        The U. S. in the U. N.   [Washington]
Dept. of State [1960]
        8 p.   illus.   24 cm.   (U. S. Dept. of
State.   Publication 7080.   International
organization and conference series, 16)

U. S. President.
        Presidential messages and state
papers; being the epoch-making national
documents of all the presidents from George
Washington to Woodrow Wilson; edited by
Julius W. Muller.   New York, Harper, 1928.
        xii, 533 p.   21 cm.

        I.   Muller, Julius W. ,   ed.

AAC 81   LEGISLATIVE BODIES

Gt. Brit. *Parliament. House of Commons.*
Hansard's Catalogue and breviate of parliamentary
papers, 1696–1834. Reprinted in facsimile, with an introd.
by P. Ford and G. Ford. Oxford, Blackwell, 1953.

xv p., facsim.: viii, 220 p.   34 cm.

Original title page reads: Catalogue of parliamentary reports, and
a breviate of their contents: arranged under heads according to the
subjects. 1696–1834. ₁London, 1836₁ Pref. signed: James & Luke G.
Hansard & sons.

1. Gt. Brit. Parliament. House of Commons—Bibl.   2. Gt. Brit.—
Government publications—Bibl.   ɪ. Hansard, James. ɪɪ. Ford,
Percy, 1894–   ɪɪɪ. Ford, Grace.

U. S. *Congress. House. Committee on Public Works.*
Water pollution control hearings on Water quality act of
1965. Hearings, Eighty-ninth Congress, first session on
H. R. 3988, S. 4, and related bills. February 18, 19, and 23,
1965. Washington, U. S. Govt. Print. Off., 1965.

v, 399 p.   24 cm.

"89–3."

1. Water—Pollution—Law and legislation—U. S.   ɪ. Title.

65–60997

Library of Congress   ₁2₁

AAC 83   COURTS

U.S. Emergency Court of Appeals.
Rules, as adopted May 14, 1949,
effective May 16, 1949.   Washington,
U.S. Govt. Print. Off., 1949.
iii, 25 p.   24 cm.

U.S. Navy.
    The naval nuclear propulsion
training program. [Catalog of
information.   Washington, 1960]
    30 p.   illus.   26 cm.

U. S. *Army air forces.*
    The official guide to the Army air forces: AAF. A directory,
almanac and chronicle of achievement. New York, N. Y.;
Simon and Schuster [1944]

    vii, [1], 380 p. incl. front., illus., plates (part col.) ports., diagrs. 22ᶜᵐ.

U.S. Marine Corps. 1st Division.
    Chosin Reservoir; First Marine
Division: November 1-December 15
[1950.   Washington, U.S. Govt. Print.
Off., 1951]
    10 p.   illus.   26 cm.

    1. KOREAN WAR, 1950-1953.
I. Title.

Permanent International Altaistic Conference. *5th, Bloomington, Ind., 1962.*
    Aspects of Altaic civilization; proceedings of the Fifth
Meeting of the Permanent International Altaistic Conference held at Indiana University, June 4-9, 1962. Edited by
Denis Sinor, assisted by David Francis. Bloomington, Indiana University [1963]

    ix, 263 p. illus. 22 cm. (Indiana University publications. Uralic
and Altaic series, v. 23)
    English, German, or French.
    Includes bibliographies.
    1. Ural-Altaic tribes.   I. Sinor, Denis, ed.   II. Indiana. Univer-
sity.   III. Title.   (Series: Indiana. University. Uralic and Altaic
series, v. 23)

    DS17.P4   1962   572.894   63-63140
    Library of Congress   [3]

AAC 93   DIOCESES, ETC.

Protestant Episcopal Church in the U.S.A.
     Niobrara(Missionary District)
     Report of the missionary bishop of
Niobrara.   New York, 1907.
     83 p. plates. 26 cm.

AAC 95 A   CORPORATE ENTRY FOR POPE

Catholic Church. Pope, 1775-1799
     (Pius VI)
     Breve apostolico de Pio Sexto, y
estatutos generales para la ereccion y
gobierno de las custodias de misioneros
fransiscos observantes de propaganda
fide en las provincias internas de
Nueva Espana.   Madrid, 1781.
     Microfilm copy.

     1. FRANCISCANS IN MEXICO.

AAC 98   LOCAL CHURCHES, ETC.

New York. Trinity Church.
     Churchyards of Trinity Parish in the
City of New York, 1697-1947. Published
in observance of the 250th anniversary
of thefounding of Trinity Church.
Enl. ed.   ⌐New York, 1955⌐
     85 p. illus., maps. 22 cm.

     1. NEW YORK(CITY)--CEMETERIES.
2. EPITAPHS--NEW YORK(CITY) I. Title.

AAC 99   CERTAIN OTHER CORPORATE BODIES

Baltimore. Museum of Art.
2,000 years of calligraphy; a three-part exhibition organized by the Baltimore Museum of Art, the Peabody Institute Library ₁and₁ the Walters Art Gallery, June 6–July 18, 1965. A comprehensive catalog. ₁Compiled by Dorothy E. Miner, Victor I. Carlson, and P. W. Filby₁ Baltimore, 1965.

201 p. illus., facsims. 28 cm.

California. State College, *Fresno. Bureau of Business Research and Service.*
Bureau of Business Research study.

₁Fresno?₁

v. 29 cm.

Detroit. *Public Schools.*
Alcohol, narcotics and tobacco. Pub. by authority of the Board of Education. ₁Rev. ed.₁ Detroit, 1947.

108 p. illus. 23 cm. (*Its* Publication no. 230)

Includes bibliographies.

1. Alcohol—Physiological effect. 2. Narcotics. 3. Tobacco—Physiological effect.   I. Title. II. Series.

HV5060.D46   1947   612.01446   48–1794*

Library of Congress   ₁2₁

AAC 102   WORKS WRITTEN BEFORE 1501

Chanson de Roland.   English.
        The legend of Roland.   Translated from
modern French after the Oxford manuscript by
Maurice Tessier.   With illustrations by
Christiane Grandsaignes.   Paris, F. Lanore,
1947.
        xxi, 133 p.   illus.   23 cm.

Arabian nights.   English.
        The book of the thousand and one nights;
Arabian love tales.   Rendered into English by
Powys Mathers.   London, Folio Society,
1949.
                ix, 245 p.   illus.   23 cm.   (Classics
of the East series)

Nibelungenlied.   English
        The Nibelungenlied.   Translated from
the German by Werner Hahaan.   With introductory notes and glossary.   London, Macmillan, 1959.
        283 p.   18 cm.

AAC 108   GENERAL RULE FOR THE BIBLE

Bible. English. Authorized. 1959.
  The Holy Bible; authorized King James
version. Edited by John Sterling.
Drawings by Horace Knowles.   London,
New York, Collins' Clear-type Press, 1959.
  xv, 256 p. illus. 20 cm.

  I. Stirling, John Featherstone, ed.
II. Knowles, Horace, 1899-1957, illus.

Bible. *O. T. Daniel* III. *English. 1965. Authorized.*
  Shadrach, Meshach, and Abednego. From the Book of
Daniel. Illustrated by Paul Galdone. New York, Whittle-
sey House [°1965]

  32 p. illus. (part col.) 26 cm.

Old
Rule   ⟶

  I. Galdone, Paul, illus. II. Title.

Bible. O.T. Isaiah. Hebrew. 1949.
  Isaiah; Hebrew text & English
translation with an introd. and commentary,
by I.W. Slotki.   London, Soncino Press,
1949.
  xiv, 337 p. 24 cm.   (Soncino books
of the Bible)

  1. BIBLE. O.T. ISAIAH--COMMENTARIES.
I. Bible. O.T. Isaiah. English. 1949.
II. Slotki, Irael Wolf, ed. (Series)

AAC 119   LITURGICAL WORKS

Catholic Church.   Liturgy and ritual.   Missal.
     St. Paul Daily missal; with the latest   Old
masses, new mass rubrics, and the new Holy   ← Rule
Week liturgy, by the Daughters of St. Paul.
With introd. by J. Alberione.   Boston,
St. Paul Editions, 1959.
     1608 p.   illus. , music.   18 cm.

Protestant Episcopal Church in the U. S. A.
     Liturgy and ritual.
     [Book of common prayer]
     The book of common prayer, and
administration of the sacraments and other
rites and ceremonies of the Church, according
to the use of the Protestant Episcopal Church
in the United States of America; together with
the Psalter.   New York, Church Pension
Fund [1945?]
          lvii, 611 p.   20 cm.
     I. Bible.   O. T.   Psalms.   English.
Great Bible. 1945.

IV. Verification

Verification is the process of proving bibliographically
whether or not a book, serial, pamphlet, etc. really exists.
Has a particular author written a particular book with a particular title published by a particular publisher in a particular place at a particular time? This is an important process because requests for material often have inaccurate
bibliographical details. The author's name may be mis-
spelled; the title may be garbled; the publisher, place of
publication or the date may be inaccurate. By consulting a
bibliography which contains a citation for the particular title
in question, any inaccuracies may be discovered. Careful
practice of verification will help to avoid the purchase of
unwanted duplicates for a library's collection.

In order to use a bibliography to verify a title, author,
etc., it is necessary to know the bibliographical characteristics of a book. There may be as many as eight different
forms of the title, for example: title-page title, sub-title,
alternative title, cover title, binder's title, half-title,
running title, caption title. Other elements involved in the
accurate identification of a particular edition of a title are
the series, the edition, the imprint, the collation, and the
size and gathering of the book.

The traditional sources of bibliographical verification
include national and trade bibliographies, national library
catalogs, and retrospective bibliographies. The American
Book Publishing Record (BPR), the Cumulative Book Index
(CBI), and the National Union Catalog (NUC) are three
commonly used sources in American libraries. The NUC
and the BPR both give complete information for catalog
cards. The CBI and the BPR both may be approached by
main entry, title, and subject, while the NUC can only be
approached by main entry. Books in Print and the Publishers' Trade List Annual may also be used in the verification process, although neither give complete cataloging
information. Three major foreign sources are the catalogs
of the British Museum and the Bibliotheque Nationale and

the British National Bibliography.   In addition, other national bibliographies may be used.   Biographical dictionaries
and directories may also be used to verify personal names
of authors.

Name Authority Cards

Name Authority cards are prepared in order to establish the correct main entry heading for a particular
author.   Pseudonyms, shortened forenames, and variations
in surnames are all brought together under one heading by
name (or author) authority cards.

STEP ONE: Book cataloged

Prepare a card with the following information from
the title page of the book being cataloged.

Book cat.

    (1)   Dodie Smith

                                (2) I Capture the Castle

                                  (3) 1948

(1)   Author's name as on title page

(2)   Title of book (shortened if necessary)

(3)   Date of publication.

STEP TWO: Verification of author

Consult the verification source or sources to be used for this particular author.   (CBI is one of the most common sources of verification.)

1)   List the source and date on the card below the Book Cat. line.

2)   Place the verified name at the top of the card in inverted form followed by available birth and death dates.

3)   If the author is verified, place the first check under the Book Cat. line before the source of verification. (Note: this is the only necessary element for verification.) Second, if the author's dates are found, place a lower case "d" at the third space from the first check.   Third, if the title of the book is found in the source of verification, place a second check after the author's check.   Fourth, if the particular book being cataloged is listed in the source, place a third check between the second check and the abbreviation "d".

4)   Indicate any necessary cross references in the lower left-hand side of the card.

Smith, Dorothy Gladys, 1896 —

Book cat.   Dodie Smith
✓✓✓ d   CBI   1943 - 46
    x Smith, Dodie
                    I Capture the Castle
                                1948

STEP THREE: Verification of additional names

Any additional names (joint authors, editors, transla-
tors, illustrators, etc.) on the title page which the cataloger may wish to use as added entries for a particular
book must also be verified in the above manner.   In addition, the following line must appear above the title line on
the name authority card: a. e. for the verified main entry.
This means that the initial name, i. e. the main entry
usually, should be verified before the added entries.

Steed, Ruth

Book cat.   Ruth Steed, illus.
   ✓   CBI   1943 - 48
   ✓   CBI   1949 - 52

a.e. For   Smith, Dorothy Gladys, 1896 -
              I Capture the Castle
                           1948

STEP FOUR: Completion of name authority card

1)   If the author's name in the Book Cat. line
matches completely with the verified form of the author's
name, cancel or remove the entire "Book Cat." line.

2)   If the verified form does not match, retain the
entire Book Cat. line.

3)   Type the card for the name authority file.

Smith, Dorothy Gladys, 1896-

Book cat.   Dodie Smith
√√√ d.   CBI 1943-48

x Smith, Dodie

                             I capture the castle
                                    1948

Steed, Ruth

                        CBI 1943-48
                        CBI 1949-52

           a. e. for Smith, Dorothy Gladys, 1896
                        I capture the castle
                              1948

Subject Authority Cards

Example:

CATALOGS, CLASSIFIED

sa	Classification--Books
x	Catalogs, Classed
	Classed catalogs
	Classified catalogs
xx	Classification--Books
	Shelf-listing (Library science)

LC Subject Headings
7th ed.

Series Authority Cards

Example:

CAMBRIDGE UNIVERSITY PRESS LIBRARY
EDITIONS

_____ Series added entry

_____ No series added entry

_____ Catalog together

_____ Catalog separately

IV.   Verification: Outline

A.   Introduction

B.   Sources of bibliographic verification

    1.   National bibliographies

    2.   Trade bibliographies

    3.   National library catalogs

    4.   Retrospective bibliographies

    5.   Other enumerative bibliographies

C.   Name authority cards

    1.   Information from the title page of the book

    2.   Verification of the author

        a.   Sources
            (1)   CBI
            (2)   LCPC & NUC
            (3)   BPR, PW
            (4)   BM, BN, and BNB
            (5)   Other National Bibliographies
            (6)   Biographical dictionaries and directories
               (a)   DAB, DNB
               (b)   WW, WWA, CA, etc.
        b.   Recording of data

    3.   Verification of additional names

    4.   Completion of card

IV. Verification: Readings

Basic Readings

Jennett, Sean. The Making of Books. 4th ed. rev. New
   York: Praeger, 1967.
   Pp. 328-385.

Mann, Margaret. Introduction to Cataloging and the Classification of Books. 2d ed. Chicago: American Library Association, 1943.
   Pp. 12-30.

Stokes, Roy. The Function of Bibliography. London:
   Andre Deutsch, 1969.
   Pp. 9-69.

Wynar, Bohdan S. Introduction to Cataloging and Classification. 3d ed. Rochester, N.Y.: Libraries Unlimited, 1967.
   Pp. 15-18.

Enrichment Readings

Bowers, Fredson. Principles of Bibliographical Description.
   New York: Russell & Russell, 1962.

_____. Bibliography and Textual Criticism.
   Oxford: Clarendon Press, 1964.

Esdaile, Arundell. Manual of Bibliography. Revised by
   Roy Stokes. 4th rev. ed. London: Allen & Unwin,
   1967.

Lowy, George. A Searcher's Manual. Hamden, Conn.:
   Shoe String Press, 1965.
   Pp. 39-44; 75-99.

McKerrow, Ronald B. An Introduction to Bibliography for
   Literary Students. Oxford: Clarendon Press, 1927.

V.   The Computer and the Cataloging Process

A series of experiments extending over nearly two decades has at last determined the requirements in hardware and software for making the cataloging process as automated as it will ever be.   In these experiments, much has been learned about the cataloging process, about centralized cataloging, and about the distinction between clerical and professional work.   Now it is possible to distinguish four levels of operation: first, the computer, which can only do what it is programmed to do, and can accomplish this with speed and efficiency which repay the cost only when the operations are to be repeated over and over again without change.   This is the lowest level of skilled work, even though some of the operations, such as putting the information in proper sequence and arranging it for duplication, may seen to be quite sophisticated.

The second level is that of the clerical worker who prepares the copy for input in machine readable form.   This level requires little more than a knowledge of the machine: keypunch, automated typewriter, or whatever.   Rules for the input of copy can be established very strictly and the clerical personnel can be trained to follow these rules without exception.

The third level is the technical assistant who prepares the descriptive cataloging and shows what entries are to be made in standardized form.   While almost all of this work is done in accordance with definite rules, some items will seem not to fit any of the rules and must be turned over to the professional for final decision.   The form of each entry must be established correctly so that maximum usefulness of stored information can be gained.   A computerized search of titles by a given author, those in which he took some part, and those for which he served as editor or compiler, can only be achieved when the form of entry is in standardized form.

Finally, the top level is the decision making level of

the professional who reviews the work of the technical
assistant and corrects it and adds the subject analysis to
the purely descriptive part of the cataloging.   Subject analysis includes not only classification number (or numbers)
but also subject headings to serve as access to these numbers.   Problems of form of entry must be resolved as
well.   The sequence of operations, then, is from technical
assistant to professional to clerical to computer.   Trial
print-outs will be reviewed by the professional as a final
check on the whole procedure.

To the knowledge of the authors, no system exists
which utilizes a computer to capacity for cataloging purposes.
The requirements are such that a single library on its own
budget could probably not afford to utilize a computer as
the card catalog is employed, although this is technically
feasible for a group of libraries operating within a quite
wide area.   It is doubtful that any great saving of time and
money would result from a completely computerized cataloging system serving several large libraries.   Experience
has shown that the resulting savings are soon required for
improved service.

The experiments, even though not complete, have
made it apparent that several traditional ideas of cataloging
are inessential, even in a mechanized or partly mechanized
system.   That is, even the most primitive cataloging process, one with all cataloging done within the library and
all cards prepared locally and individually, is fastest and
costs least when the operations are broken down to several
steps which can be accomplished by members of the cataloging department with different levels of skill--from the
typist who prepares the card for duplication to the head
of the department who makes final decisions only on the
most problematic of materials, designs the flow of work,
and who maintains the quality of the finished product.   The
professional does as little writing as possible, almost no
descriptive cataloging, and very little proofreading.   His
time is devoted almost entirely to the problems of subject
analysis.   The technical assistant accomplishes almost all
the descriptive cataloging, except for the rare book which
fits none of his rules.   He establishes the form of entry,
but there is no need to choose a main entry if the title is
selected as the unit entry.

Where automated typewriters are employed, the title
entry as unit entry is acceptable and permits automatic

reproduction of the cards without the need for further proof-reading. While it is true that there are many titles which are identical or similar, some that are nondescript, such as "Complete Works," and some that are misleading, the title entry card does not become less useful than the main entry as unit entry. Unit entry assumes that all other entries will contain the complete bibliographic description, so that no entry needs to be "main"; that is, contain full bibliographic description so that it can be abbreviated under other entries. As indicated above, the form of entry must be clearly established so that the work of maintaining authority files is still necessary. However, very much more freedom is permitted in making entries, especially when the card catalog is considered a temporary device and the book catalog is the permanent record of the holdings. Even in book catalogs, the title as entry serves better than the main entry, especially as information increases in volume so that individual authorship becomes less important and subject analysis becomes the only access to the material in the library except for the scholars who specialize in a given subject area. These individuals may find access easier by author, but other users will rely on the subject analytic system.

The Marc I and Marc II projects at the Library of Congress further established that information could be accumulated gradually so that the cataloging process can begin in a computerized system when the material is ordered and be complete when the material is in hand. Further, the end of a main entry system means that material can be organized largely by subject so that various kinds of material are very readily treated by the same rules: pictures, motion pictures, slides, phonorecordings, and so forth. It is now apparent that, rather than trying to make the computer fit the operations of cataloging which were established fifty to seventy-five years ago, we achieve best results by making the operations fit the particular program designed for the computer to obtain results not possible before.

Further, even the Marc I and Marc II programs are more complicated than is necessary if a simplification of procedure accompanies the change to computerized cataloging. Just how these developments will affect such old problems as centralized or cooperative cataloging is unknown at present, but it seems likely that cataloging-in-source, or cataloging which accompanies the published book, will take into account the distinction between descrip-

tive cataloging based on the book itself and the need for subject analysis, so that a project now under discussion in the
United States will most likely follow the lead of Russia,
where the experiment has been tried. Classification numbers and subject headings will be supplied along with the
established form of possible entries. This would leave the
cataloging department of a library with even less need for
professional catalogers, except to decide on the extent to
which the library will follow the suggestions given in the
book. Much more time can be spent not on cataloging the
entire work but on making analytics which will be useful
to the particular library.

These new, and challenging, possibilities leave some
catalogers in doubt and afraid. In libraries where the cataloger must do his own typing and where a perfect card for
reproduction is the responsibility of a professional (who
may be a good cataloger but a poor typist), the division of
work is considered somewhat degrading to the profession.
But in libraries where it has been tried, there is a great
increase in speed of production, and "arrearages" may be
reduced and volume of books cataloged increased sizably.
All the efforts at cooperative and centralized cataloging
work toward the goal of cataloging a book only once. Now
it is realized that if the rules of description are made
simple and precise enough, if all the elements of the description are derived from the book itself, and if there is
no subjective decision to be made about one entry as opposed
to another, then centralized cataloging may be more expensive than local cataloging, especially when a computer
stores information until needed and produces it on demand.

V.   The Computer and the Cataloging Process: Outline

I.   Early investigations

    A.   MARC I

    B.   Florida Atlantic University

    C.   Chicago Campus, University of Illinois

II.   Later investigations

    A.   MARC II

    B.   Book Catalog preparation

III.   Standards of computer input

    A.   Sequentiality and linearity

    B.   Multi-dimensional access

    C.   Storage routines and retrieval

IV.   Procedures for computer input

    A.   Order file

    B.   Receipt of material

    C.   Completion of bibliographic record (cataloging)

    D.   Organization of subject approach (classification)

    E.   Updating and correcting the record

V. The Computer and the Cataloging Process: Readings

Basic Readings

U. S. Library of Congress. Information Systems Office. MARC Manuals used by the Library of Congress, Prepared by the Information Systems Office, Library of Congress. Chicago: Information Science and Automation Division, American Library Association, 1969.

Enrichment Readings

Avram, H. D. "MARC II and COBOL," Journal of Library Automation, 1:261-73, December 1968.

_____. "MARC Program Research and Development," Journal of Library Automation, 2:242-65. December 1969.

"MARC Special Institute (Denver, Colorado), A Report on the Proceedings of Sessions 2 & 3 of the MARC Special Institute held in Denver, Colorado, August 12 & 13, compiled by Frank S. Patrinostro," LARK Reports, 30:1-19, 1968.

"MARC Special Institute (Seattle, Washington), A Report on the Marc Special Institute held in Seattle, Washington, July 18, 19, 1968, compiled by Catherine MacQuarrie," LARK Reports, 29:1-20, 1968.

Markuson, Barbara. "A System Development Study for the Library of Congress Automation Program," Library Quarterly, 36:197-233, July 1966.

Seminar on the Organization and Handling of Bibliographic Records by Computer, Newcastle-upon-Tyne, 1967. Organization and Handling of Bibliographic Records by Computer. Edited by Nigel S. M. Cox and Michael W. Grose. London: Archon Books, 1967.

U. S. Library of Congress. Information Systems Office.
The MARC Pilot Project, Prepared by Henriette D.
Avram. Washington: 1968.

_____. Serials, A MARC Format, Working Document.
Washington: 1969.

U. S. Library of Congress. RECON Working Task Force.
Conversion of Retrospective Catalog Records to
Machine-Readable Form, A Study of the Feasibility of
a National Bibliographic Service, Prepared by the
RECON Working Task Force, Henriette D. Avram,
Chairman. Washington: Library of Congress, 1969.

United States of American Standard Institute. Subcommittee
on Machine Input Records, SC-2. Special Project on
Data Elements. The Identification of Data Elements in
Bibliographic Records, by Ann T. Curran and Henriette D. Avram. n.p., 1967.

PART 2: SUBJECT ANALYSIS

VI.   Introduction to Subject Analysis

Most activities in our daily lives deal with decision-
making processes concerned with orderly (or disorderly)
systems.   Some of these systematic arrangements are made
by others and we must conform to them; some we make
ourselves.   For instance, in a grocery store or a department store we must discern what sort of systematic arrangement or classification has been used to display the merchan-
dise.   In these instances materials are often classified by
type and then by size.   Further, the paint in a hardware
store may be arranged by type of paint, or brand, or color,
or purpose, or even by size of container.   These are, of
course, systems of classification based on physical properties.   We, too, develop our own classification systems in
our homes.   We are involved in a systematic distribution
or arrangement of the groceries in the cupboard or pantry
and in the refrigerator.

The foregoing examples have all dealt with systematic
decisions concerning physical properties of items; in addition, we often must choose arrangements or classifications
in regard to abstract qualities such as good or evil, sound
or unsound, pros and cons, assets and liabilities, or even
love and hate.   We work within structured organizations.
We live within an organized family unit.   Even our leisure
time may be very neatly systematized for us by ourselves,
by our wives or husbands, our children, our friends, or by
our vast American entertainment industry.   We live with
and by hundreds of different classification systems which
effect us every day.

Classification in general is defined by the Oxford
Dictionary as: "1) The action of classifying.   2)   The result of classifying; a systematic distribution or arrangement,
in a class or classes."[1]   S. R. Ranganathan presents this
concept of classification in the following, "Classification,
in this sense, is still highly potent, though it originated
with the primitive man.   It continues to take man further
and further from his primitive state.   Its potency increases

with his increase in his power of abstraction--with the
evolution of the cortex of the brain. Indeed most intellectual problems are ultimately problems of classification
in the first sense. "[2]

From these statements a definition of library classification may be evolved: "A systematic scheme for the
arrangement of books and other material according to subject or form. "[3] W. C. Berwick Sayers states both the purpose and definition in the following. "The foundation of the
library is the book; the foundation of librarianship is classification. Without classification no librarian can build up a
systematic library; one, that is to say, which represents
adequately the field of human learning as it is recorded in
books. "[4] E. Wyndham Hulme presents a practical definition: "Book classification is a mechanical time-saving
operation for the discovery of knowledge in literature.
Books are our theme; and the discovery of knowledge in
books by the shortest route our aim and object. "[5]

This is how Ranganathan writes about library classification:

> What, then, is 'library classification'? It is the
> translation of the name of the subject of a book in-
> to a preferred artificial language of ordinal num-
> bers, and the individualisation of the several books
> dealing with the same specific subject by means of
> a further set of ordinal numbers which represent
> some features of the book other than their thought-
> content. The first of these ordinal numbers is
> called the Class Number of the book. The second
> ordinal number is called its Book Number. It is
> usual, in practice, to separate the book number
> from the class number by a space, or to write
> one below the other. The class number and the
> book number together constitute the Call Number
> of a book. The call number fixes the position of
> a book relative to the other books in a library. [6]

He continues his definition to the verbal form "to classify":
"To determine the specific subject of a piece of writing or
kindred material and to translate the name of the specific
subject into its class number in accordance with the preferred scheme of classification. "[7]

As librarians we may be concerned with the physical

properties of research materials. We may classify all our
materials alphabetically by the author or creator. For instance, the naval memoirs of Admiral George Dewey would
be shelved beside the educational theories of John Dewey
followed by the classification tables of librarian Melvil
Dewey and the campaign speeches of Tom Dewey. Or we
may choose the name, i. e. the title, of the book as our
systematic arranging element. An alphabet of titles might
give us such unlikely bedfellows as Faith of our Fathers,
Family Planning, Famous Educators, and Fanny Hill.
Obviously, however, we cannot alphabetize by both author
and title without having at least two copies of every piece
of material. Further, we may select some physical property
such as color, date of publication, size, or binding for our
arrangement. All the red books could be together; all the
green books together, etc. In fact, many interior decora-
tors make use of just this sort of classification to create a
tasteful wall of books; they will even purchase books by the
foot or by the yard. We can even disregard all the properties of the book and classify it by a number which shows
when the book was received or what its location in the library will be where one book is simply put after another.
In fact, each of these classifications might serve the needs
of a single user or group of users--but obviously we can't
keep rearranging the material according to the whims and
fancies of each user. To paraphrase Lincoln, we can
please some of the users all of the time but not all of the
users all of the time. Rather, we have chosen to classify
material by subject, i. e. the abstract qualities.

Such classifications are called natural classifications
because they depend upon the language of the book and the
subject matter which it conveys. So far, research in classification has determined only four types of natural classification, though there may be others as yet undiscovered. Two
of these are basically unidimensional. These are sequential
classification, which is simply a list without any attempt of
broader or narrower distinctions, and hierarchical classification, in which the narrower terms are contained within
broader descriptors. Hierarchical systems depend upon the
most specific description possible for the items classified,
and systematic arrangement so that the breadth of coverage
is equivalent to the subject matter classified. Multi-dimen-
sional classifications provide for greater freedom and
greater approximation to the subject matter. The faceted
classification always has a limited number of descriptors
arranged in some order, and is therefore a kind of fixed

field classification.   An associative classification may have several descriptions limited with special signs, so that it constitutes a free field arrangement.

Research in classification has continued from the earliest days of libraries but its purpose is simply to serve the user, just as research in medical science is conducted for the purpose of curing the sick.   Classification may be used for catalogs as well as for the items classified.   In modern open-stack libraries the classification serves to arrange books where the user interested in a particular subject will have the greatest likelihood of finding the material he can use.   Closed stack libraries, where books are arranged by fixed location, make use of a classified catalog which achieves the same object by a different method.   Classified catalogs are more often used in Europe than in the United States, though examples abound in all parts of the world. Whether it is the book or a card that is marked with the notation of a natural classification, the purpose is to assist the user in finding related material rapidly.   However, no classification so far has been able to bring together all the possible relationships of the information sources classified. Most modern classification systems group by subordination to traditional academic disciplines.   Classification brings like or similar academic disciplines and their subordinates together, separating them from unlike or different disciplines.   This concept leads naturally into two approaches to classification, philosophical and utilitarian.   Philosophical classification attempts to create a library classification which is really a complete classification of knowledge--not knowledge as it is represented in printed material.   Such a system of classification may be called philosophical, knowledge, or scientific classification.   The second approach to classification attempts to be a system based on the books themselves, not simply the knowledge represented by them. This type of classification may be called book classification, bibliographical classification, practical classification or utilitarian classification.

Philosophers, from the time of Aristotle onwards, have observed that some fields are adequately described by different words, and that a group of specific terms can be identified with one general term.   The natural language we use aids in classification just as classification aids memory.   While artificial and accidental classifications depend upon some feature of the book itself or of the library receipt of the book, natural classification depends upon the use of natural language in a specially controlled form to limit meanings and provide specificity.

References

1. Oxford Universal Dictionary. (New York: Oxford University Press, 1962), p. 320.

2. S. R. Ranganathan, Classification and Communication. (Delhi: University of Delhi, 1951), pp. 113-114.

3. A. L. A. Glossary. (Chicago: American Library Association, 1943), p. 30.

4. W. C. Berwick Sayers, A Manual of Classification for Librarians and Bibliographers. 3d ed. rev. (London: Grafton & Co., 1955), p. 9.

5. E. Wyndham Hulme, Principles of Book Classification. (London: The Association of Assistant Librarians, 1950), p. 2.

6. S. R. Ranganathan, Elements of Library Classification. (London: The Association of Assistant Librarians, 1959), p. 2.

7. Ranganathan, Classification and Communication, op. cit., 35.

A.   Types of Classification

   1.   Abstract: Not related to subject content

      a.   Artificial
         (1)   By title
         (2)   By author
         (3)   By publisher, date of imprint, size, or binding
      b.   Accidental
         (1)   By accession number
         (2)   By fixed location, may include size

   2.   Natural: based on subject content

      a.   Introduction
      b.   Unidimensional
         (1)   Hierarchical.
         (2)   Sequential.
      c.   Multidimensional
         (1)   Associative.
         (2)   Faceted.

B.   The Object of Classification and All Subject Analysis

   1.   Traditional academic classes

      a.   Philosophical classification
      b.   Utilitarian or book classification

   2.   Natural subject categories

      a.   Natural classificatory language
      b.   Controlled vocabulary
         (1)   Form
         (2)   Meaning

   3.   Sayer's Rules

   4.   Merrill's Code for Classifiers

VI. Introduction to Subject Analysis: Readings

Basic Readings

Daily, Jay E. "Abstract Classification," Encyclopedia of
Library and Information Science. New York: Marcel
Dekker, 1968. Vol. 1:12-16.

_____. "Subject Headings and the Theory of Classifi-
cation," American Documentation, 7:269-274, October,
1957.

Sayers, W. C. Berwick. A Manual of Classification for
Librarians and Bibliographers. Rev. ed. London:
Grafton, 1955, Pp. 1-88, 234-242.

Enrichment Readings

Mann, Margaret. Introduction to Cataloging and the Classification of Books. 2d ed. Chicago: American Library Association, 1943. Pp. 31-43; 86-99.

Perreault, Jean M. "On Bibliography and Automation; or,
How to Reinvent the Catalog," Libri, 15:287-339,
1965.

Sayers, W. C. Berwick. An Introduction to Library Classi-
fication: Theoretical, Historical and Practical, with
Readings, Exercises and Examination Papers, 9th ed.
London: Grafton, 1954. Pp. 1-68.

Shera, Jesse H. and Egan, Margaret. The Classified Catalog, Basic Principles and Practices. Chicago: American Library Association, 1956. Pp. 22-63.

Wynar, Bohdan S. Introduction to Cataloging and Classification. 3d ed. Rochester, N.Y.: Libraries Unlimited, 1967. Pp. 165-182.

VII. Library of Congress Classification

1. Introduction

The Library of Congress classification was originally
designed and intended as a utilitarian system for the use of
the Library of Congress only. In 1901, Herbert Putnam,
the Librarian of Congress at that time, wrote:

> The system devised has not sought to follow strictly
> the scientific order of subjects. It has sought
> rather convenient sequence of the various groups,
> considering them as groups of books, not as groups
> of mere subjects. [1]

To some extent, the classification developed as a group of
special or individual classifications universal in scope.
Berwick Sayers in his Canons of Classification calls it "...
not a complete subjective compendium of knowledge but
rather a series of large special classifications. "[2] The
British librarian, Ernest Savage, points out:

> Books are readily grouped by the LC because its
> tables are hypothetic in origin and empirical in
> development; the first draft of them was revised,
> as the classing proceeded, to offer hospitality to
> the towering quantity of books that had to be accom-
> modated. Books were not rammed into a 'true
> order of the sciences' but insinuated into affined
> groups in which they, and any published later,
> would give support to each other; a great library,
> well-classed on this plan, could adopt the fasces
> as its symbol with more propriety than the state
> which Mussolini gummed together with castor oil and
> blood. The bibliographical foundation of the LC is
> traceable throughout the schedules. Here is a book
> difficult to class. But, no. The right place, the
> heading picked to describe it, is there. [3]

2. The Format

a. The schedules

The schedules for LC classification comprise 29 individual volumes for the main classes and subclasses.   A full
set of schedules contains nearly 7,000 pages and costs over
$60.00.   The individual schedules are:

1) A: General works, Polygraphy.

2) B, pt. 1, B-BJ: Philosophy.

3) B, pt. 2, BL-BX: Religion.

4) C: Auxiliary Sciences of History.

5) D: General and Old World History.

6) E-F: American History.

7) G: Geography, Anthropology, Folklore, Manners
and Customs, Recreation.

8) H: Social Sciences.

9) J: Political Science.

10) KF: Law of the United States.

11) L: Education

12) M: Music and Books on Music.

13) N: Fine Arts.

14) P-PA: Philology, Linguistics, Classical
Philology, Classical Literature.

15) PB-PH: Modern European Languages.

16) PG, in part: Russian Literature.

17) PJ-PM: Languages and Literature of Asia,
Africa, Oceania, America, Mixed Languages,
Artificial Languages.

18) PN, PR, PS, PZ: Literature (General), English and American Literature, Fiction in English, Juvenile Literature.

19) PQ, pt. 1: French Literature.

20) PQ, pt. 2: Italian, Spanish, and Portuguese Literatures.

21) PT, pt. 1: German Literature.

22) PT, pt. 2: Dutch and Scandinavian Literatures.

23) Q: Science.

24) R: Medicine.

25) S: Agriculture, Plant and Animal Industry, Fish Culture, and Fisheries, Hunting Sports.

26) T: Technology.

27) U: Military Science.

28) V: Naval Science.

29) Z: Bibliography and Library Science.

Besides these 29 schedules, there are presently in use two supplements, one partial index, and the outline of the classes. The supplements are for: 1) PA containing Byzantine and modern Greek literature; and 2) T, Technology. The partial index is for subclasses P-PM, languages and dialects only. A total of 33 physical volumes comprise the LC schedules.

The individual schedules are kept current by: 1) the quarterly Additions and Changes to LC Classification; 2) the addition of supplementary pages to the later printing of an edition of an individual schedule; and 3) periodic new editions of the individual schedules. Both the quarterly Additions and Changes and the supplementary pages are printed on leaves, i. e. with alternate pages blank, to allow the possibility of clipping and tabbing into the original schedules. The new edition of an individual schedule includes all additions and changes in the main sequence of the schedule. Class Q is already in its fifth edition. Classes T and Z

are in fourth editions.   Classes A, E-F, G, H, L, N, R,
S and U are all in third editions.   The remaining classes
are all in second editions with the exception of the entire
Class P which still is in its first edition.

Each schedule has a similar if not identical format.
The usual elements making up each schedule are: 1) a
prefatory note, containing a brief history of the schedule as
well as concise remarks on the scope of schedule; 2) a
synopsis, consisting of a list of all double letters covered
in the schedule; 3) an outline, in greater detail than the
synopsis of the portion of the classification covered in the
schedule; 4) the schedule, containing the main classification
tables; 5) any necessary auxiliary tables; 6) a detailed index; and 7) any supplementary pages of additions and
changes to the schedule.   All 29 schedules do not have
auxiliary tables; some do not have an outline (e. g. Subclasses PN, PR, PS, PZ); and some do not have an index
(e. g. Subclass PQ, pt. 1 or pt. 2).   Usually, if there is
no index to a schedule, there is an extensive outline at the
beginning of the schedule.

b.   Notation

LC call numbers, like Dewey Decimal Classification
call numbers, consist in general of two principal elements,
a class number and an author number, to which may be
added symbols designating a particular title and a particular
edition.   For example, the third edition of Richard D. Al-
tick and Andrew Wright's Selective Bibliography for the
Study of English and American Literature has the following
call numbers in LC classification and Decimal Classification.

	LC Classification	Dewey Classification
Class number:	Z2011	016. 82
Author number:	. A4	A468s
Publication date used to indicate later edition	1967	1967

The main classes in LC are designated by single
capital letters, the subclasses by two capital letters (except in classes E-F and Z) and the divisions and sub-

divisions by integral numbers in ordinary sequence ranging
from 1 to 9999, which may be extended decimally.   In the
example above, the class number "Z2011" in LC means a
general bibliography of English literature as does the Decimal Classification number "016. 82. "

Additional numbers used in an LC call number consist
of one or two Cutter or author numbers.   A Cutter number
consists of an initial letter followed by Arabic numerals.
In the example above ". A4" is the author number in LC
while "A468" is the author number if the work is classed
in the Decimal Classification.

3.   Use of LC Printed Cards

One major factor influencing many libraries to convert
to LC classification is the existence of the complete LC
call number on the LC printed cards.   This LC number
has a great advantage over the suggested Decimal Classification number on the LC printed card.   The Decimal Classification number is only a class number and not a whole call
number.   One disadvantage of complete acceptance of the
whole LC call number is the problem of assigning original
Cutter numbers to those works for which LC cards have
not been printed; obviously a complete Library of Congress
shelf list is not available to libraries using LC classification.   Further, all LC call numbers should be carefully
checked before being automatically accepted.   Typographical
errors do occur; some material may need to be reclassified.
The classifier will find the Library of Congress Catalog of
Books Represented by Library of Congress Printed Cards,
its successor, the National Union Catalog, and the Library
of Congress Catalog, Books: Subjects invaluable aids in
establishing and verifying actual Library of Congress classifying practice.

References

1.   Herbert Putnam.   "Manual: Constitution, Organization,
       Methods, etc. , "   In Report of the Librarian of Con-
       gress for the Fiscal Year Ending June 30, 1901.
       (Washington: Govt. Print. Off. , 1901), p. 234.

2.   W. C. Berwick Sayers, Canons of Classification. . . (Lon-
       don, Grafton, 1915), pp. 127-161.

3. Ernest Albert Savage, <u>Manual of Book Classification and Display for Public Libraries.</u> (London, Allen & Unwin, 1946), pp. 15-52.

2.   Simple Auxiliary Tables

    a.   Ten Number Countries
    b.   Two Number Countries
    c.   One Number or Cutter Number Countries

3.   Complex Tables for Individual Authors in Literature

    a.   Authors with Forty-eight Numbers
    b.   Authors with Eight or Eighteen Numbers
    c.   Authors with One Number or a Cutter Number

4.   Complex Tables of Geographical Divisions

    a.   Twenty Number Countries
    b.   Ten Number Countries

5.   An Example of a Special Problem in Table Use

VII. Library of Congress Classification: Readings

Basic Readings

Immroth, John Phillip. A Guide to Library of Congress Classification. Rochester, N.Y.: Libraries Unlimited, 1968. Pp. 9-159.

Perreault, Jean M., "Making LC Teachable," Library Journal, 93:4269, November 15, 1968.

Supplemental Readings

Grout, Catherine W. Explanation of the Tables Used in the Schedules of the Library of Congress Classification, Accompanied by an Historical and Expanatory Introduction. New York: Columbia University, School of Library Service, 1940.

Hoage, A. Annette Lewis. "The Library of Congress Classification in the United States: A Survey of Opinions and Practices, with Attention to Problems of Structure and Application," Unpublished Doctoral dissertation, Columbia University, 1961.

LaMontage, Leo E. American Library Classification with Special Reference to the Library of Congress. Hamden, Conn.: Shoe String Press, 1961.

Schimmelpfeng, Richard H., ed. The Use of the Library of Congress Classification. Proceedings of the Institute on the Use of the Library of Congress Classification Sponsored by the American Library Association, Resources and Technical Services Division, Cataloging and Classification Section. Edited by Richard H. Schimmelpfeng and C. Donald Cook. Chicago: American Library Association, 1968.

Indexes

Boston University. Libraries. Index to the Classed Catalog of the Boston University Libraries; A Relative
Index Based on the Library of Congress Classification.
Compiled by Mary Darrah Herrick. 2d ed., rev. and
enl. Boston: G. K. Hall, 1964. 2v.

Dewton, J. L. "Subject Index According to Library of
Congress Classification," Library of Congress In-
formation Bulletin, 8:12-13, December 27, 1949-
January 2, 1950.

Edinburgh. Public Library. Subject and Name Index of
Books Contained in the Libraries. 3d ed. Edinburgh:
Published by Edinburgh Public Libraries Committee,
1949.

Nitecki, Andre. Index to the Library of Congress Classification Outline. Syracuse: Syracuse University,
School of Library Science, 1967.

U. S. Library of Congress. Subject Cataloging Division.
Subject Headings Used in the Dictionary Catalogs of
the Library of Congress. 7th ed. Washington: Govt.
Print. Off., 1966.

Abridgements

Rovelstad, Betsey. "Condensation of the Library of Congress M Classification." [n. p.] : 1953.
This is an abridgement of Class M: Music which
was reprinted in 1963 as Supplement No. 34 to Music
Library Association's Notes.

Perry, F. C. "The Library of Congress Classification
Adapted for School Libraries," School Library Re-
view, 7:68-73, 1938. This is an adaptation of
Classes D, G, H, J and P.

Tiffy, Ethel. "Library of Congress Classification Simpli-
fied for Use in the Smaller College Library." Unpublished Master's thesis, Columbia University, 1935.
This is simply an abridgement of the history Classes
C, D, and E-F. An abstract of this thesis appears
in the ALA Cataloging and Classification Yearbook,
5:95, 1936.

Printed Cards

U. S. Library of Congress. <u>Catalog of Books Represented by Library of Congress Printed Cards</u>. . . Ann Arbor, Mich. : Edwards, 1942-1955. 191v. (Title varies.)

_____. <u>The National Union Catalog</u>: a Cumulative Author List Representing Library of Congress Printed Cards and Titles Report by Other American Libraries. Jan. 1956--. Washington: Govt. Print. Off. , 1956--. (Title varies.)

_____. <u>Library of Congress Catalog, Books: Subjects, 1950-1954.</u> Ann Arbor, Mich. : Edwards, 1955. 20v.

_____. _____, <u>1955-1959.</u> Paterson, N. J. : Pageant Books, 1960. 22v.

_____. _____, <u>1960-1964.</u> Ann Arbor, Mich. : Edwards, 1965. 25v.

_____. _____, <u>1965--</u> Washington: Govt. Print. Off. , 1965--

CLASS A

Give appropriate classification numbers for titles listed below. Consider the title the main entry if no personal author is given.

1. Encyclopedia Americana.

2. New International Encyclopedia.

3. La Grande Encyclopedie. (French)

4. Latviju Maza Enciklopedija. (Latvian)

5. Compton's Pictured Encyclopedia. (Children's encyclopedia)

6. Webster's New International Dictionary.

7. Larousse, Pierre. Nouveau Petit Larousse Dictionnaire. (French)

8. Oxford English Dictionary.

9. Beckmanns Neues Welt-Lexikon mit Welt-Atlas. (German dictionary)

10. Readings in Museum Techniques, by Jackson.

11. Introduction to Museum Management, by Aldrich.

12. "Museums and Monuments." (A periodical published by UNESCO. Does not have references to a particular country)

13. Guide to the Museums of Oslo, Norway, compiled by Oscar Sturli.

14. Handbook to the Museums of Kiev, Russia, compiled
     by Sergie Gogol.

15. Handbook of Museums in the United States, compiled
     by Clarkson.

16. The Swedish Museums: a Handbook and Guide, by
     Tharalson.

17. The Museums of Moscow, compiled by Vorontsov.

18. "Modern Museums." (A periodical published in the
     United States)

19. Handbook to the Museums of Luxembourg, by Thiers.

20. The History of the Metropolitan Museum of Art, by
     Williams.

21. "News Notes." (A serial publication of the Denver
     Art Museum)

22. Guidebook to the Philadelphia Museum of Fine Arts.
     (Published in 1961 by the museum itself)

23. Annual Reports of the Denver Museum of Natural
     History.

24. Whitaker's Almanack. (British: began publication in
     1869)

25. Canada Year Book. (Published since 1905)

26. Canadian Almanac and Directory for the Year 1847-.
     (Published since year indicated)

27. Thrum's Hawaiian Annual and Standard Guide. (Pub-
     lished since 1875 by the Honolulu Star-Bulletin.
     Main entry under title)

28. Handbook of Jamaica. (Published since 1881. Main
     entry under Jamaica Tourist Association)

29. Centralinis Statiskos Buras. (A Lithuanian Yearbook)

30. Apercu Statistique. (Published since 1931 by the
     Luxemburg Office de Statistique)

SCHEDULE PN, PR, PS, PZ

Give the appropriate classification numbers for the titles listed below.

1. The Complete Works of Lord Byron, edited by George W. Cooke.

2. The Complete Poems of Lord Byron, 1904.

3. The Life of George Gordon, Lord Byron, by Mrs. Sutherland Orr.

4. A Handbook to the Works of Byron, by George W. Cooke.

5. Don Juan, by Lord Byron, edited by Charlotte Porter.

6. A Concordance to Byron, compiled by Sidney James.

7. The Complete Poems of William Butler Yeats, 1933.

8. The Complete Works of William Butler Yeats, 1908.

9. The Green Helmet and other Poems, by W. B. Yeats, 1910.

10. Deirdre, a play, by W. B. Yeats, 1907.

11. Reveries over Childhood, an autobiographical work, by Yeats.

12. W. B. Yeats Letters to Bernard Shaw.

13. William Butler Yeats, a critical study; Forrest Reid.

14. W. B. Yeats, an authorized biography, by Joseph Hone.

15. Finnegan's Wake, by James Joyce. 1957.

16. A Skeleton Key to Finnegan's Wake, by Joseph Campbell and Henry Morton Robinson.

17. Poems Penyeach, (poems), by James Joyce.

18. James Joyce, a biography, by Herbert Gorman.

19.   James Joyce's Ulysses, a Study, by Stuart Gilbert.

20.   James Joyce, a Critical Study, by Harry Levin.

CLASS H

1.   "The Chartist Movement in the British Isles," by
      Webb.

2.   "The Italian Laborer in West Germany," by Herzmark.

3.   "Who's Who in Canadian Labor."

4.   "The Parisian Working Class after the Revolution of
      1848," by Egard.

5.   "Labor Conditions in the Mexican State of Yucatan,"
      by Morelos.

6.   "History of Labor and the Laboring Classes in British
      Honduras," by Smith.

7.   "Keir Hardy; British Labor Leader," by Munro.

8.   "Foreign Labor in Britain Today," by Wilson.

9.   The Annual Report of the Minister of Labor in Greece.

10. The Annual Report of the Director of the Child Labor
      Bureau in the Labor Department of the Greek Govern-
      ment.

11. A statistical handbook on labor conditions in Guatamala,
      compiled by Asiento.

12. A labor handbook and directory for British Honduras,
      compiled by Garst.

13. The Annual report of the Department of Labor in
      Albania.

14. The Annual Report of the Department of Labor in
      Malta.

15. A History of Labor in the Arab countries.

16. A history of Communism in Europe, by Goldmark.

17. "French Communism, an introduction and explication,"
     by Sartre.

18. "The Communist Party in the City of Rome," by Sforza.

19. A history of Communism in Germany, by Ulbricht.

20. "The Communist Menace in the United States," by
     Hargis.

SCHEDULE B

1. Readings in Persian philosophy, compiled by Inman.

2. A history of Chinese philosophy, by Russell.

3. Ancestor worship in Chinese philosophical thought, by
    Cartwright.

4. Idealism in Indian philosophy, by Peters.

5. The works of Mencius, 1901.   (In Chinese)

6. The works of Mencius translated into English, by
    Cartwright, 1905.

7. The complete works (published in 1864) of Han Fei.
    (In Chinese)

8. The works of Han Fei translated in German, by
    Wincklemann, 1921.

9. A biography of Han Fei, by Baer.

10. Selections from the works of Han Fei in Chinese, 1904.

* *

(From the "B" Schedule, pt. 1)

B
350-398   Plato.   (Table 1)
   . . .
      368   Crito

(Note: Plato in the schedule
is actually worked out with
a slight variation from
Table 1. For our purposes
we will use Table 1 as

385   Symposium   applicable to the numbers
                                    for Plato).

* *

11.   A biography of Plato, by Jowett.

12.   A dictionary to the works of Plato, by Leopold.

13.   The collected works of Plato, without commentary,
      published in 1891.   The text is in Greek.

14.   Selections, in Greek, from the works of Plato, com-
      piled by Edgerton.

15.   The complete works of Plato translated into German
      by Goethe.

16.   The complete works of Plato translated into Russian
      by Tolstoi.

17.   A criticism and interpretation of the "Symposium" by
      Jowett.

18.   A translation of the "Crito" into French by Gide.

19.   Text of the "Symposium" in Greek, published in 1963.

20.   "Plato today; a criticism and interpretation," by
      Kopel.

VIII. Dewey Decimal Classification

A. Introduction

Melville Louis Kossuth Dewey was born on December 10, 1851 and died on December 26, 1931. He graduated from Amherst in 1874 and became assistant librarian there following graduation. His accomplishments include being an organizer of Library Journal in 1876 and its first editor; an organizer of the American Library Association, the Spelling Reform Association, and the American Metric Bureau, all in 1876; further, he organized the first library supply company, the Library Bureau, the following year, and the first library school at Columbia in 1887, which he moved to Albany in 1889. However, he had one additional accomplishment which most concerns us here. In 1876 he issued the first edition of his own system of classification, the Decimal Classification.

Dewey's outline was based on that of William T. Harris of the St. Louis Public Schools in 1870. Harris had used an inversion of Baconian order. Bacon's classes were: 1) History evolving from the human faculty, memory; 2) Poesy, evolving from imagination; and, 3) Philosophy, evolving from reason. Harris inverted this order to: 1) Science, including philosophy and religion; 2) Art, including fine arts, poetry, and fiction; and, 3) History, including geography, civil history, and biography. Dewey's original element was claimed to be the Relativ Index. This is the opposite of a specific index which was then commonly used. In a specific index the entry of an item is in only one place in the index. In a relative index an item may appear in related places under more than one subject. Today this system is widely used in most public and school libraries in America. Currently, the system is in its 17th edition (which has caused nearly as much controversy as the 15th edition). There is also an abridged version of Dewey which is now in its 9th edition.

B. Basic concepts

The basic outline of this classification is that all knowledge is divided into ten broad subject classes from 000 to 999.

The first summary of Dewey shows this breakdown by the main classes.   The second summary shows a more detailed outline by the subclasses of the tens.   The third summary is the most detailed outline which is arranged by the ones.   Throughout the classes, subclasses, divisions, and subdivisions of Dewey there is an obvious hierarchical structure of the general to specific.   For example 300 is the Social sciences; 370 is a subclass of the social sciences, Education; 371 is The school; 372 is Elementary education; 373 is Secondary education; 374 is Adult education; with 374.1 as Self-education, 374.2 Group education, 374.21 Special interest groups, 374.22 Reading and discussion groups, 374.26 Use of radio, 374.27 Use of motion pictures and television, 374.28 Community centers for adult education, 374.29 Institutions and agencies; with 374.291 Private and 374.292 Governmental, which is further subdivided into 374.2922 Federal and national, 374.2923 State and provincial, and 374.2924 County and local.   Further, the notation of Dewey follows a definite pattern.   A Dewey number must always have three digits as well as any desirable decimal extensions.   The length may become very great as for example Ralph C. James' biography of Hoffa, Hoffa and the Teamsters, classed at 331.88113883240924.

C. Specific concepts

A Dewey number may be subdivided in four ways: by standard subdivisions, by chronological subdivisions, by geographical subdivisions, and by subject subdivisions.   The standard subdivisions make use of mnemonic devices which aid the user to remember certain physical or philosophical forms of a subject.   These devices are: 01 Philosophy and Theory; 02 Miscellany (including compends, manuals, outlines); 03 Dictionaries; 05 Serial publications; 06 Organizations; 07 Study and teaching; 08 Collections and anthologies; and 09 Historical and geographical treatment.   These subdivisions may be attached at the end of any number or may be considered for attachment only when directed by the tables.   In the second volume of Dewey there are additional decimal extensions for more detailed applications; e.g. 0202 may be used to mean outlines--a subdivision of miscellany.

The use of these numbers is clearly marked in the tables.
Chronological or period subdivisions are usually fully developed within the tables.   Geographical subdivisions are
given in the second volume in the area table.   The numbers
in the area table may be attached to the end of any number
as directed by the tables.   Subject subdivisions are always
fully developed in the tables as the above example of Adult
education demonstrates.

In order to establish an internal alphabetical order of
books within a Dewey Decimal class number many libraries
use Cutter numbers as the second part of a call number.
These Cutter numbers are taken from a table of predeter-
mined numbers based on common names in the Roman alphabet.   There are three different Cutter tables which are
widely used in American libraries.   These are Cutter two-
figure tables, Cutter three-figure tables and Cutter-Sanborn
three-figure tables.   A full discussion of the use of these
tables may be found in the basic and enrichment readings
for this unit.

Once a Cutter number has been determined, the next
element of the call number may be an initial or combination
of initials called the work marks.   If the Cutter number
stands for the author's last name, as it usually does, the
work mark will probably stand for the title of the book.
This work mark is usually represented in lower case form.
The difference of edition may also be shown in the call
number.   The easiest method for showing a different edition is simply to add the date of the different edition as
the next element of the call number following the Cutter
number and work mark.

Although most Cutter numbers stand for the author's
name, the Cutter numbers for biography usually stand for
the subject of the biography rather than the author of the
biography.   If the Cutter number does stand for the subject
of the biography, the work mark may stand for the author
of the biography rather than the title.   This method allows
all the biographies about an individual person to stand on
the shelf in one place.

It should be clearly understood that all Cutter numbers
must be adjusted to each library's own shelf list.   The Cutter numbers taken from any of the Cutter tables are only
approximations and must be adjusted in actual practice.

VIII. Dewey Decimal Classification: Outline

A. Introduction

B. Basic concepts

   1. Decimal division

   2. Hierarchical classification structure

   3. The notation

C. Specific concepts

   1. Subdivisions

      a. Standard subdivisions
      b. Chronological subdivisions
      c. Geographical subdivisions
      d. Subject subdivisions

   2. Use of the area table

   3. Other mnemonic devices

      a. Form divisions for languages
      b. Form divisions for literary genres
      c. Nationality division for both languages and
          literatures
      d. Others

   4. Cutter numbers

      a. Use of the table
      b. Work marks
      c. Difference of edition
      d. Translations
      e. Biography
          (1) Classed with subject
          (2) Classed in general biography

       (a)   920's

       (b)   B

f.   Criticisms of individual authors

g.   Bibliographies, concordances and dictionaries of individual authors

h.   Adjustment of Cutter numbers to the shelf list

VIII.   Dewey Decimal Classification: Readings

Basic Readings

Wynar, Bohdan S. Introduction to Cataloging and Classification. 3d ed. Rochester, N. Y.: Libraries Unlimited, 1967. Pp. 183-206.

Enrichment Readings

Barden, Bertha R. Book Numbers; a Manual for Students,
with a Basic Code of Rules. Chicago: American
Library Association, 1937.

Cutter, Charles Ammi. Explanation of the Cutter-Sanborn
Author-Marks, Three-Figure Tables. Revised by
Kate Emery Jones. Northampton, Mass.: Kingsburg
Press, 1935.

Dewey, Melvil. Dewey Decimal Classification and Relative
Index. Edition 17. Lake Placid Club, N. Y.: Forest
Press, 1965. Pp. 63-105 contain Dewey's introduction.

Hinton, Frances. "Dewey 17: A Review," Library Resources & Technical Services, 10:393-402, Summer,
1966.

Kephart, Horace. "Classification," Papers Prepared for
the World's Library Congress Held at the Columbian
Exposition. Edited by Melvil Dewey. Washington:
Govt. Print. Off., 1896. (Reprint of Chapter IX of
Part II of the Report of the Commissioner of Education
for 1892-93.) Pp. 861-897.

Lydenberg, H. M. "Dewey, Melvil," Dictionary of American
Biography. New York: Charles Scribner's Sons, 1944.
Vol. 21, Supplement 1, pp. 241-243.

Metcalfe, John. Dewey's Decimal Classification, Seventeenth
Edition: An Appraisal. Sydney: James Bennet, 1965.
(Australian Library Pamphlet Series, no. 2)

Tauber, Maurice.   Technical Services in Libraries: Acqui-
    sitions, Cataloging, Classification, Binding, Photo-
    graphic Reproduction, and Circulation Operations.
    New York: Columbia University, 1954.   Pp. 177-232.

DEWEY DECIMAL NUMBERS

I. Give the correct meaning for each of the following numbers; indicate any numbers that are not in effect in the abridged edition.

1. 708 _____

2. 808 _____

3. 970. 1 _____

4. 961. 03 _____

5. 948. 07 _____

6. 620. 1 _____

7. 909 _____

8. 220. 1 _____

9. 301 _____

10. 321. 04 _____

11. 620. 1003 _____

12. 942. 05 _____

13. 942. 005 _____

14. 070. 01 _____

15. 220. 3 _____

16. 300. 1 _____

17.   321. 004 _____

18.   970. 03 _____

19.   991. 4002 _____

20.   861. 004 _____

21.   946. 005 _____

22.   985. 01 _____

23.   978. 801 _____

24.   620. 09 _____

25.   620. 9 _____

STANDARD SUBDIVISIONS

I.   Write the correct abridged Dewey number in each blank.

1.   _____   A dictionary of physics

2.   _____   An outline of history

3.   _____   Essays about literature

4.   _____   A periodical of art

5.   _____   The philosophy of religion

6.   _____   The study and teaching of arithmetic

7.   _____   An educational society

8.   _____   A collection of writings about science

9.   _____   The philosophy of music

10.   _____   A history of philosophy

11.   _____   A dictionary of United States history

12.   _____   A collection of writings about chemistry

13. _____ The history of language

14. _____ A collection of American poetry

15. _____ A periodical of drawing

16. _____ The study and teaching of art

17. _____ An outline of zoology

18. _____ Essays about philosophy

19. _____ A scientific society

20. _____ A society of chemists

21. _____ An encyclopedia of clothing

22. _____ Essays about American literature

23. _____ A dictionary of music

24. _____ Study and teaching of agriculture

25. _____ The history of sculpture

ANALYSIS

Analyze as many of the following numbers as possible using the 17th edition.

016. 929799995

155. 849591

264. 0300903

220. 59691

338. 47677310994

362. 6124

387. 00061519

420. 71273

492. 4983

599. 01593

570. 6273

636. 08960149

658. 4007152

791. 43090916

808. 838109034

917. 12210403

940. 487430924

979. 8009172

918. 30403016

IX. Subject Headings

Since the early nineteenth century, access to books by
means of a formalized list of subjects has been a desirable
feature of a catalog. The development of subject heading
lists in the United States developed from the rules set down
by Cutter in the four editions of his Rules for a Dictionary
Catalog. As lists of subject headings were developed by
the American Library Association, the Library of Congress
and by Minnie Earl Sears, the advantage of standardized
lists became apparent. Subject headings as foreshadowed
in the earliest catalogs of the sixteenth and seventeenth cen-
turies had none of the problems found in modern subject
catalogs.

These derive from the purpose of subject analysis.
A catalog is useful if it provides information on the holdings
of a library to those who have some identifying features of
books they know of, and to those who simply know the subject areas of their interest. To require that everyone
know all the books before he could use any of them would
defeat the purpose of the library. Access by subject is
essential, and the access is easiest for the user when the
subject headings are in his own language and in terms that
he already knows. When the nature of language was less
well understood, it seemed obvious that a good noun or
noun phrase would supply every want.

However, various rules to control terminology are
necessary and various means to show interrelationships between words are essential. The development of data processing, utilizing computer technology for the retrieval of
information, has put particular importance on subject analysis in natural language. English, as a lingua franca, that
is a language which has crossed ethnic and cultural bound-
aries to the extent that any word may be readily borrowed
and utilized, presents problems of organization in a subject catalog, and these became apparent only as thesauri
for information retrieval files were developed. The pres-
ence or lack of an "s," indicating plural, may change the

175

meaning of a term, as in words derived from verbs such
as "drawing" and "drawings."

Further problems of terminology occur when two different terms may refer roughly to the same thing, as in
"automobiles" or "cars." One may be chosen as a subject
heading but reference must be made to the one term chosen
from those which are not chosen. Further, boundary of
words is still a problem, so that the only valid definition
of a word is purely typographical. Many phrases are
roughly equal to a single word in some cases, so that
the single word may be selected as the subject heading.
However, there are no one word equivalents for the larger
number of terms, and as technology advances there tend
to be fewer words than we need to name all the parts of
all the tools that modern science employs. Finally, words
change meaning sometimes with great speed, so that a term
with one area of meaning may need to be limited by other
words as time passes. An established list which limits the
possibilities of variation and produces consistency is essential for any retrieval system which aims at something better
than haphazard retrieval of desired information. Such a list
must be at once highly standarized in its terminology and
in the relationships between terms, and yet be flexible
enough to allow for growth of terminology and change of
meaning.

Various syndetic devices have been used to assist the
user from a heading which does not quite fit the subject
for which he is searching, to the heading which more nearly
states the object of his search. Modern lists commonly
employ see also references which require see-also-from
references in order to function adequately. A growing body
of evidence suggests that the desired standardization and
flexibility can only be achieved in a classified system, and
the method of classification must be fairly precise and
readily expanded if the list is to have any degree of per-
manence. Indeed, the problem of subject headings is fo-
cussing attention, once again, on the classified catalog as
the best way of providing subject access to information in
a large or highly specialized system.

A.   Introduction to Subject Headings Used by the Library
      of Congress

In 1914 the Library of Congress issued the first

edition of Subject Headings Used in the Dictionary Catalogues of the Library of Congress. This list was followed by a second edition in 1919, a third in 1928, a fourth in 1943, and a fifth in 1948. The sixth edition was published in 1957 and the seventh in 1966. The Library of Congress list is kept current by monthly, bi-monthly, semi-annual and annual supplements.

LC subject headings, just as is the case with LC classification, are developed for the actual holdings of the Library of Congress. LC subject headings appear on LC printed cards. LC subject headings may be used with either LC classification or any other classification system, especially DC.

Large public libraries, college and university libraries and some special libraries use LC subject headings. Many smaller libraries selectively use LC subject headings--especially the ones on LC printed cards. Although LC subject headings and Sears subject headings are often used in the same catalog, neither system is completely compatible with the other. Many adjustments are required if both are used together. It is not recommended to use more than one subject headings list in any library situation.

B. Basic Types of LC Subject Headings

One definition of subject headings is, "Subject Headings are terms denoting subjects under which material is entered in a catalog." This concept may be amplified by a discussion of the structure of LC subject headings. The following types of main subject headings are used by the Library of Congress: 1) simple nouns; 2) qualified nouns; and 3) phrase headings.

1. Simple Nouns

This type of headings consists of a simple noun either in singular or plural form. Examples are "Botany" or "Airports."

2. Qualified Nouns

This type of heading consists of a noun and an adjective or adjectival noun. These headings may be called adjectival or modified headings. The very nature of the

English language allows many different possibilities for this
type of heading. The modifier may be simply a common
adjective, e. g. --"Agricultural credit"; the modifier may be
a proper adjective, e. g. --"Brownian movements"; the modifier may be an ethnic or geographic adjective, e. g. --"Jewish libraries"; the modifier may be a common or proper
noun in the possessive case, e. g. --"Nurses' aides"; or,
modifier may be an adjectival noun, e. g. --"Play schools. "
Further, this type of heading may take the form of an inverted adjectival heading if the noun is felt to be more important than the adjective, e. g. --"Harmony, Keyboard" or
"Propaganda, American. " A third type of qualified noun
heading is the use of a parenthetical statement following
the noun, e. g. --"Programming (Mathematics)" or "Per-
fection (Ethnics). "

3.   Phrase Headings

Phrase headings consist of one or two nouns with or
without modifiers connected by a preposition or conjunction.
These include: 1) simple phrase headings such as "Divine
right of kings"; 2) inverted phrase headings (used when the
second element is considered to be more important) such
as "Groups, Theory of"; 3) compound phrases consisting of
two or more coordinate elements joined by a conjunction,
e. g. --"Medicine and religion"; and 4) phrase headings
qualified by parenthetical elements, e. g. --"Promoters of
Justice (Canon law). "

C.   Types of Subheadings

There are four basic types of subheadings for LC subject headings. These subheadings are designed to subdivide
individual subject headings. A subheading is separated
from the subject heading it subdivides by a dash.

e. g.   France--History.

"History" is the subheading. The four types of subheadings
are: 1) general form subdivisions; 2) geographic subdivisions;
3) chronological subdivisions; and 4) special topic subdivision.

1.   General Form Subdivisions

This type of subheading may be used with any subject heading in the LC list. These subheadings are used to

indicate the physical or philosophical form or arrangement
of an individual book.   The General Form Subdivisions are
listed at the beginning of the LC Subject Headings List.

2.   Geographic Subdivisions

This type of subheading is used when a subject is
limited to a geographic or political area.   The qualifiers
"direct" or "indirect" must appear following the subject
heading in the LC subject headings list if geographic subdivisions are to be used.

    e. g.   Methane industry (Direct)
    or   Physical geography (Indirect)

A subject heading that may geographically subdivide "directly" may use any geographic area for that subdivision.

    e. g.   Methane industry--El Paso Co. , Colo.

An "indirect" geographic subdivision interposes the name of
the country or state between the heading and the place within
that country or state to which the subject matter is limited.

    e. g.   Physical geography--Colorado--El Paso Co.
    not   Physical geography--El Paso, Colo.

3.   Chronological Subdivisions

Period or time subdivisions may be used either directly or indirectly.   Some headings for a subject may be
divided chronologically in a direct fashion.

    e. g.   Arithmetic--Before 1846.
             Arithmetic--1846-1880.

Geographic headings subdivide chronologically in an indirect
fashion.   The following terms may be interposed between
the geographic heading and the chronological subdivision.

    --Church history.
    --Description and travel.
    --Economic conditions.
    --Economic policy
    --Foreign relations.
    --History.
    --History, Military.

--History, Naval.
--Politics and government.
  (Politics--if used under name of a continent.)
--Religion.
--Social life and customs.

    e. g.   Hungary--Economic conditions--1918-
            Holy Roman Empire--History--1648-1804.
            Ireland--History--Civil War, 1922-1923.
            Italy--Church history--18th century.

    4.   Special Topic Subdivisions

    Each heading may have special topic subdivisions appropriate to the particular heading or similar headings only.

    e. g.   Dressmaking--Pattern design.
    or   Kimonos--Pattern design.

D.   Proper Names as Subject Headings

    Proper names, either individual or geographic, may be used as subject headings. Although most proper names are not included in the list of the Subject Headings Used in the Dictionary Catalogs of the Library of Congress, any proper name may be used.

    1.   Individual Names

    An individual name may be used as a subject heading for a critical, historical or biographical work about the individual person. Individual names may be either real or imaginary persons, corporate bodies, individual works of literature or art, sacred books and anonymous classics, animals which are identified by name, structures and any other individual entries bearing a proper name.

    a.   Personal names

    The properly verified form of personal names is to be used for the subject heading. If the literature about a person is voluminous, the heading form of the personal name may be subdivided by the form of material. Shakespeare, Lincoln, Napoleon, Washington, and Richard Wagner are all fully developed as examples in the LC list. Also the cataloger should be aware that the Library of

Congress omits the dates of well known authors when used
as subject headings. Further the cataloger using LC printed
cards should be aware that the Library of Congress will
usually omit author subject headings for autobiographies.
If a library has a divided catalog, it is important that a
personal name subject heading be made for the author of an
autobiography.

b.   Corporate Bodies

ALA Rules must be followed for subject headings of
accounts of the origin and development, analyses and discussion of the organization and function of corporate bodies.
However, the name of the corporate body should be used
for works about that body specifically, not for works which
are limited to the physical plant.

> e. g.   Colorado.   Adams State College, Alamosa.
>   for works on the history, organization, and
>   activities of the college as a state school.
> but   Adams State College, Alamosa, Colorado.
>   for works about the school itself.

c.   Biblical, Imaginary, Mythological, and Legendary Names

Names of such beings may be used as subject headings
in the same fashion as those of real persons.   The form
of biblical names should follow the form of the name in the
Authorized (King James) Version of the Bible.   References
from other forms, including the forms used in the Douay
version should be made.

> e. g.   Elijah, the prophet.
> and   refer from Elias, the prophet.

For the forms of imaginary, mythological and legendary
names, the best known English form of the name should be
given preference with references from other forms.

d.   Proper Names of Other Kinds

Ships, famous horses, buildings, individual monuments,
etc. may serve as the subject of a book.   The proper names
of these other kinds may then serve as subject headings.
Usually such names will be qualified by a parenthetical ex-
pression describing their nature.   "References should be

made from the next broader category of heading within
which the subject matter covered by the specific heading
would fall. "

    e. g.   Titanic (Steamship).
          Refer from Shipwrecks.
          Man o'War (Race horse).
          Refer from Horse-racing.

e. Individual Works of Literature

An individual work of literature may require a subject
heading if the work is the subject of a criticism or commentary. This type of subject heading consists of the
name of the author followed by the form of the title used
as a filing title.

    e. g.   Shakespeare, William.
          Hamlet.
    Or to save space,
          Shakespeare, William. Hamlet.

Note the use of "Hamlet" and not the full title of the play,
"The Tragedie of Hamlet, Prince of Denmarke. "

f. Sacred Books and Anonymous Classics

Anonymous Classics require subject headings if they
are the subject of criticisms or commentaries. The form
of this heading is to follow exactly the form used for
anonymous classics according to the usage of the Library
of Congress. The same usage is basically true of a subject heading for a Bible or a part of it. However, in
Bible subject headings, the elements of the main entry
form beyond the name of the part are not used.

    e. g.   Bible. O. T. Isaiah.
    but not Bible. O. T. Isaiah. English. 1914.
            Authorized.

Subheadings are often used with Bible subject headings.

    e. g.   Bible. O. T. Isaiah--Commentaries.
    or   Bible. N. T. --Concordances.

2. Geographic Names

The Library of Congress uses the form of geographic names as established by the U. S. Geographic Names Board. Whenever possible a purely geographic name is preferred to a political one, i. e. the form of the name an area is continued to be known by even after a new political name is adopted.

e. g.   Russia.
          not Union of Soviet Socialist Republics
          or Russian Socialist Federated Soviet Republic.
        Great Britain.
          not United Kingdom.
        United States.
          not United States of America.

Geographic subject headings may be used whenever a geographic area is the subject of an account or other work. Geographic headings may be qualified in three different fashions: a) generically, b) geographically, and c) politically.

a.   Generic Qualifiers

Proper names of natural geographic features usually consist of a specific term and a generic term.

e. g.   English Channel.
        Rocky Mountains.

If the generic term precedes the specific term, the inverted form is used.

e. g.   Mexico, Gulf of.
        Dover, Strait of.

b.   Geographic Qualifiers

If the name of a place or locality is not readily identifiable, the name of a major or larger geographic or political area is needed.   Especially for the majority of cities in the United States the state is necessary.

e. g.   Boulder, Colorado.

The Library of Congress omits the designation of state or

province or country for well-known cities.

c.   Political Qualifiers

If the same name is used for different political and/or ecclesiastical jurisdictions a qualification in parenthesis follows.

> e. g.   New York   (Archdiocese).
> New York   (City).
> New York   (Colony).
> New York   (State).

This qualification may be extended to the names or abbreviations and dates of different political regimes.

> e. g.   Russia.
> (No qualification refers to the Imperial Government prior to 1917.)
> Russia   (1917-   Provisional govt.)
> Russia   (1917-   R. S. F. S. R.)
> Russia   (1923-   U. S. S. R.)

d.   Geographic Names of the Ancient World

The geographic names of the ancient world are generally treated in a fashion similar to the personal names of the ancient world.   For Greek or Roman names use the Latin form of the name as used in standard classical dictionaries. For the names of biblical places use the form of the name as found in the Authorized Version of the Bible.

e.   Changes in Geographic Names

Although one may often use a geographic name for a country in preference to a political one, the cataloger is forced to use the various changed names of cities and localities.   As a general rule, prefer the latest form of the name; however, if the material deals with the city during the period of an earlier name, the earlier name is preferred.   This means that there must be a complete network of references from one form of the name to the others.

> e. g.   St. Petersburg.
> see also other forms of the name
> Petrograd.

Leningrad.
Petrograd.
see also other forms of the name
Leningrad.
St. Petersburg.
Leningrad.
see also other forms of the name
Petrograd.
St. Petersburg.

E. Duplicate Entry

Duplicate entry is the "entry of the same subject matter under two distinct aspects of it." Duplicate entry is used to express a mutual opposition of two interests or points of view. It is important for the cataloger to include subject headings for both forms of the duplicate entry.

e.g.   1)   U. S. -- Foreign relations -- France.
              France -- Foreign relations -- U. S.
        2)   Literature, Comparative -- French and
              German.
              Literature, Comparative -- German and
              French.
        3)   French drama -- Translations from Greek.
              Greek drama -- Translations into French.

F. Syndetic Devices

A syndetic device is one that binds together or connects. The references in a card catalog may be called syndetic devices. Entries are connected by cross references. There are three basic types of syndetic devises used in a card catalog. "See" references, "See also" references and general references are the three basic types. References to individual names and scope notes are additional syndetic devises.

1. "See" References

A "see" reference is a reference from a heading (term or Name) not used as a subject heading to the corresponding subject heading that is used.

e. g.   Blackmail.
         see
         Extortion.

         Language and languages--Religious questions
         see
         Language question in the church.

2.   "See also" References

A "see also" reference is a reference from one subject heading to another subject heading.   A "see also"
refers from a more general subject heading to a more
specific subject heading or from one coordinating subject
heading to another subject heading--but not from a specific
subject heading to a more general subject heading.

e. g.   Science.
                 see also
             Astronomy.
             Physics.

and   Astronomy.
                 see also
             Physics.

but not   Astronomy.
                 see also
             Science.

3.   General References

General references are blanket references from a
general category to the names of individual classes making
up that general category.

e. g.   Cats.
             See also names of different kinds of cats, e. g. ,
             Angora cat, Siamese cat, etc.
or   Libraries.
             See also subdivision Libraries under names of
             cities, e. g. , Chicago--Libraries.

Obviously the general reference can save space in a card
catalog.

4. References to Black Headings

This phrase recalls the period in American cataloging
when all subject headings were typed in red ink and all
main and secondary entries were typed in black ink.   A
reference to a black heading is then a reference from a
"red" heading, i. e. subject heading, to an individual name.

e. g. Architects, British.
       see also
       Wren, Sir Christopher, 1632-1723.

This form of syndetic device is not widely used today.
There are obvious problems in keeping such a reference
card current.

5. Scope Notes

Scope notes are statements indicating the subject
matter covered by a given heading.   Scope notes may state
what is included and what is excluded.   The scope notes
in the LC subject heading list may be used quite advanta-
geously in any card catalog, using LC subject headings.

e. g. Library statistics.
       Here are entered works on the compilation
       and study of statistics of libraries.   Col-
       lections of statistics are entered under
       Libraries--[local subdivision], names of
       special types of libraries, and names of
       individual libraries with subdivision Sta-
       tistics, e. g. Libraries--Wisconsin--Sta-
       tistics; Libraries, University and college--
       Statistics; New York.   Public Library--
       Statistics.

G. Physical Characteristics of the List

All main headings in the LC list of subject headings
are printed in boldface type.   All headings not used and
all subdivisions are printed in light face roman type.   Im-
mediately following the main heading is the provision for
geographic subdivision, the words (Direct) or (Indirect)
if the main heading may be subdivided geographically.   The
next element in the LC entry is the suggested class number according to Library of Congress classification.   The

fourth element is the occasional inclusion of a scope note
for the subject heading.   The references, sa, x, and xx,
make up the next element.   The symbols sa, x, and xx,
mean: sa--refer to; x--refer from; and xx--refer from.
Or sa reads down in the normal order and x and xx both
read up.   The following example demonstrates this.

        e. g.   The following is found in the subject headings
                list:
                Balloons.
                        sa   Balloon ascensions.
                        x   Military balloons.
                        xx   Airships.
                This means:
                    1)   Balloons.
                            see also
                            Balloon ascensions.
                    2)   Military balloons.
                            see
                            Balloons.
                    3)   Airships.
                            see also
                            Balloons.

The last element is normally the list of special subdivisions
available to that particular subject heading.   The following
example demonstrates all of the elements in the format of
an individual subject heading in the LC list.

        e. g.   Libraries and schools.   (Indirect)   (Z718)
                        Here are entered general works and works
                            on libraries and schools in the United States.
                        Works dealing with libraries and schools in
                            other countries are entered under Libraries
                            and schools--[country],   e. g. ,   Libraries
                            and schools--France.
                        sa   Children's literature.
                             Libraries, Children's.
                             Library Day.
                             School libraries.
                         x   Schools and libraries.
                        xx   Children's literature.
                             Libraries, Children's.
                             School libraries.
                             Schools.
                        --France.
                             Note under Libraries and schools.

H.   Auxiliary Lists

There have been five different auxiliary or special lists of subject headings and subdivisions.   The special lists of subject headings are: 1) Music Subject Headings (1952); and 2) Literature Subject Headings and Language Subject Headings (5th ed., 1926).   The auxiliary lists of subdivisions are: 1) Period Subdivisions under Names of Places (1950); 2) Subject Subdivisions (6th ed., 1924); and 3) Subject Headings with Local Subdivisions (5th ed., 1935). All of these lists may prove helpful to the cataloger interpreting LC printed cards.   However, only Period Subdivisions under Names of Places is truly necessary as a supplement to the LC list.   The material in the other lists has been incorporated into the sixth edition of the LC subject heading list.

I.   Sears List of Subject Headings

After much careful work to formulate a list of subject headings for a small library, whether school or public, Minnie Earl Sears guided three editions through the publishers in 1923, 1926, and 1933.   Isabel Stevenson Monro and Bertha Frick edited the next five editions.   Under Barbara M. Westby, the most significant change of method and structure was made when the suggested Dewey Decimal Classification, common to all the previous editions, was dropped.   Some librarians were assigning class numbers on the basis of the subject headings, and Miss Westby along with others thought this was a misuse of the system.

The Sears List of Subject Headings contains mostly simple, broad terms, using single nouns, nouns with qualifiers, and a few phrases.   The principles of subdivision by form, chronology, and geography have been followed, along with special topic subdivision as needed. Other subdivided headings are shown in bold face type as main headings.   The large number of omitted headings, with reliance on U.S., Ohio, and Chicago as key headings, indicates that the careful cataloger will be required to make many more headings in the Sears system than in the Library of Congress system.

The Sears list contains detailed instructions and examples of how the subject heading system is meant to work.   These instructions are valid for any system using

the same kind of subdivisions and syndetic devices.   Half
of each page is blank so that the cataloger has adequate
space to write in headings which are not included in the
book.   The only full elaborate syndetic structure is the
familiar see also method found in the Library of Congress
list of subject headings.   However, through the eighth
edition, a classified list was at least theoretically possible,
and an example of the grouping of headings using the suggested DDC numbers for the headings in the eighth edition
of Sears is enclosed.   The fully classified list can be
found in The Encyclopedia of Library and Information Science under the heading "Classification and Categorization."

Compared with the LC list, the Sears list is much
shorter and simpler in both the kind and number of scope
notes, the clarity of explanation, and in the clear instructions for the use of the key headings.   However, this very
simplicity argues against the use of Sears for anything but
a small library, because a great many of the terms included will be found to be too broad and general in their
coverage to serve a special library or even a medium-
sized general library.

If the list were reorganized to include both alphabetic
and classified arrangement, then the problems with the
see also structure would largely be eliminated.   Just how
this is so can be seen from a portion of the classified list
included below through the kind permission of the editors
of the Encyclopedia of Library and Information Science.
Implicit in the method is the listing of more than one classification number which has the effect of providing several
different lists of related terms.   Such a procedure, even
on an uncontrolled basis, results in better organization of
the list and makes it more useful both to the cataloger and
to the instructed user of the library.

001   Intellectual cooperation
      Learning and scholarship
002   Books
006   Cybernetics
007   Research
010   Bibliography
      Book collecting
      .78   Information storage and retrieval systems
014   Pseudonyms
015   Bibliography—Editions
      Catalogs, Publishers'
      Government publications
      Paperback books
      .73   U.S.—Government publications
      .771   Ohio—Government publications
      .7731   Chicago—Government publications
016   Best sellers
      Books and reading—Best books
      Catalogs, Subject
      .63   Agriculture—Bibliography
      .8   Literature—Bio-bibliography
      .81   American literature—Bio-bibliography
      .82   English literature—Bio-bibliography
      .8223   Shakespeare, William—Bibliography
      .91   Directories
      .92   Chicago—Bio-bibliography
      Ohio—Bio-bibliography
      U.S.—Bio-bibliography
      .973   U.S.—Bibliography
      .9771   Ohio—Bibliography
      .97731   Chicago—Bibliography
017   Catalogs, Booksellers'
      Catalogs, Classified
      Library catalogs
018   Catalogs, Booksellers'
      Library catalogs
019   Catalogs, Booksellers'
      Library catalogs
020   Libraries
      Libraries—U.S.
      Library schools and training
      Library science

021 Library service
 .2   Libraries and readers
 .3   Libraries and schools
 .4   Discussion groups
       Libraries and moving pictures
       Libraries and pictures
 .6   Bookmobiles
       Library extension
 .7   Advertising—Libraries
       Book Week
       Public relations—Libraries
 .8   Libraries and state
022 Library architecture
 .9   Library equipment and supplies
023 Librarians
       Libraries—Trustees
       Library Administration
024 Libraries and readers
025 Library administration
 .1   Library finance
 .17 Archives
       Clippings (Books, newspapers, etc.)
       Government publications
       Pamphlets
       Periodicals
 .2   Book selection
 .3   Cataloging
 .33 Subject headings
 .37 Files and filing
 .4   Classification—Books
       Classification, Decimal
 .5   Reference books
 .6   Libraries—Circulation, loans
 .7   Bookplates

IX.   Subject Headings: Outline

A.   Introduction

   1.   Brief history

   2.   Purpose

   3.   Problems in terminology

   4.   Need for an established list

   5.   Use of syndetic devices

B.   The Library of Congress list

   1.   Introduction

      a.   Brief history
      b.   Basic principles

   2.   Physical characteristics and format

      a.   Classes of headings omitted
      b.   Indirect and direct subdivision
      c.   Scope notes
      d.   Syndetic devices
      e.   General form subdivisions
      f.   Other subdivisions
         (1)   Chronological
         (2)   Geographical
         (3)   Topical
      g.   Suggested LC Classification numbers
      h.   Abbreviations used

   3.   Structure of LC headings

      a.   Simple nouns
      b.   Qualified nouns
      c.   Phrase headings

4.   Proper names as headings

   a.   Individual names
   b.   Geographic names

5.   Auxiliary lists of subject headings

C.   <u>Sears List of Subject Headings</u>

1.   Introduction

2.   Structure of headings

3.   Types of subdivisions

4.   Physical characteristics and format

   a.   Scope notes
   b.   Syndetic devices
   c.   Use of key subject headings

5.   Comparison to LC list

Subject Headings: Readings

Enrichment Readings

Daily, Jay E.   "Many Changes, No Alternations: an Analysis of Library of Congress Subject Headings, Seventh
Edition," Library Journal 92:3961-3963, November 1,
1967.

Eaton, Thelma.   Cataloging and Classification; an Introductory Manual. 4th ed.   Ann Arbor, Mich.:   Edwards
Brothers, 1967.   Pp. 139-165.

Frick, Bertha M.   "Suggestions for the Beginner in Subject
Heading Work," Sears List of Subject Headings.   9th
ed.   Edited by Barbara Marietta Westby.   New York:
The H. W. Wilson Co., 1965.   Pp. 13-29.

Haykin, David.   Subject Headings; a Practical Guide.   Washington: Govt. Print. Off., 1951.

Mann, Margaret.   Introduction to Cataloging and the Classification of Books.   2d ed.   Chicago: American Library Association, 1943.   Pp. 136-170.

Pettee, Julia.   "The Philosophy of Subject Headings,"
Special Libraries, 23:181-182, April 1932.

_____.   Subject Headings; the History and Theory of
the Alphabetical Subject Approach to Books.   New
York: The H. W. Wilson Co., 1946.

Tauber, Maurice.   Technical Services in Libraries; Acquisitions, Cataloging, Classification, Binding, Photographic Reproduction, and Circulation Operations.
New York: Columbia University Press, 1954.

Wynar, Bohdan S.   Introduction to Cataloging and Classification.   3d ed.   Rochester, N. Y.:   Libraries Unlimited,
1967.   Pp. 223-260.

Subject Headings: Worksheets

Select the best subject headings possible from: (1)
the Sears List of Subject Headings; and (2) the Library of
Congress list of Subject Headings for the following topics.
In some instances you may wish to select more than one
heading from each list.

1. British regional geology, the Thames valley

Sears _____

LC _____

2. The music of central Africa

Sears _____

LC _____

3. Readings on Chinese communism

Sears _____

LC _____

4. Marine influence on the climate of Southern California

Sears _____

LC _____

5. Planning church buildings

Sears _____

LC _____

6.   India's China policy

     Sears _____

     LC _____

7.   Historical sketch of the early schools in Denver

     Sears _____

     LC _____

8.   A career in the world of fashion

     Sears _____

     LC _____

9.   Youth employment program of the United States Em-
     ployment Service

     Sears _____

     LC _____

10. Folk dances for Jewish festivals

     Sears _____

     LC _____

11. Animal Behavior

     Sears _____

     LC _____

12. Italian cookery for the American kitchen

     Sears _____

     LC _____

13. Introduction to Cataloging and Classification

     Sears _____

     LC _____

INDEX

201